THE VATICAN COUNCIL AND ALL CHRISTIANS

☿ *The Vatican Council and All Christians*

by CLAUD D. NELSON

Foreword by Roswell P. Barnes
Epilogue by Edward Duff, S.J.

ASSOCIATION PRESS   NEW YORK

The Vatican Council and All Christians

———

Copyright © *1962*
National Board of Young Men's Christian Associations

———

Association Press, 291 Broadway, New York 7, N. Y.

—

Publisher's title stock number: 1495

Library of Congress catalog card number: 62-16876

Foreword

Pageantry, pomp, and power will probably dominate the early photographic representation of the Second Vatican Council. Being the obvious and dramatic features, they can be reported easily.

But the Council will be much more than a colorful spectacle. It will be an important historical event, not only for Roman Catholics but also for all Christians.

To interpret the news reports of the Council will require some understanding of its background. We who are not Roman Catholics should appraise it in terms of its own purposes and nature rather than according to our own wishes as to what it might do and be. However, our own wishes are not irrelevant. Indeed, the Pope has set up a Secretariat for Promoting Christian Unity, one of the functions of which is to establish lines of communication for "separated brethren" to express their concerns regarding Christian unity as well as to obtain information. We are, of course, free to be critical; but we should be reasonable.

We can anticipate what the Council's agenda and procedures will be like if we become familiar with the general features of the preparatory commissions and the general organization as described in preliminary announcements.

We should have some ideas as to what the Council may accomplish. To expect too much is unfair, contributing to later disillusionment and frustration. To expect too little is to manifest at best a lack of faith, or at worst, antagonism. We should try to avoid excesses of either optimism or pessimism.

Or to put this point in another way, we should keep in mind, on the one hand, the intransigent problems of Christian history—the long record of controversies and traditional tensions—and, on the other hand, the power of the Holy Spirit to break old bonds and to lead into new paths.

This book is most timely. Although it had to be sent to press before the preparations for the Second Vatican Council were completed, it contains the necessary background information to enable the reader to interpret the news with wisdom and appreciation. The essential facts from history and the present relationships among the major branches of the Christian Church are accurately recorded.

The author is careful to distinguish between reporting facts and giving his own interpretation of them. When he moves into the future, his educated guesses are fair and logical. He is not so much trying to forecast as to stimulate the reader's imagination and suggest the points for which he should be alert.

Dr. Nelson is extraordinarily well equipped, by virtue of his special competence and experience, to give us this background briefing and interpretation. Some twenty years of experience in Rome as a YMCA secretary in association with Protestants, Eastern Orthodox, and Roman Catholics enabled him to develop facility in the Italian language and familiarity with Vatican practices. He has long been committed to furthering mutual understanding among Christians of various traditions based upon loyalty to truth rather than the sentimental good will of neutralism which emanates from religious indifference.

Especially important for such writing as this is the author's practice of distinguishing scrupulously between facts and rumors. Perhaps this habit was cultivated while he was reading law as a Rhodes Scholar at Oxford. However acquired, it is a characteristic which justifies confidence in the integrity of this book.

Although this reviewer has neither competence nor authority to attest to the substance of this book in detail, he commends it gratefully and enthusiastically as a timely, reliable, and highly useful contribution to the understanding of one of the major events in the history of the Christian Church in our day.

Roswell P. Barnes
Executive Secretary in the U.S.A.
of the World Council of Churches

Contents

1. The Significance of the Second Vatican Council

Pope John XXIII announced on January 25, 1959, that he would call a general, or "ecumenical," council of the Roman Catholic Church. More than once he has referred to the inspiration, like the sound of a bell, which he said came to him while he was at prayer during the 1959 Chair of Unity Octave. There were many cardinals, he said, who were "better fitted" than he to become pope. But, he added, if God wished him to be chosen, it was surely in order that he might bring about the union of the churches. In announcing the council, Pope John remarked that after two months or so of his pontificate, people were beginning to wonder what would be its character. It is clear that he wishes to be remembered as the Pope of the Council—the first, be it noted, since the promulgation of the doctrine of papal infallibility in 1870.

It May Bring Christians Closer Together

His general thesis regarding the council, perhaps best expressed in the encyclical "Ad Petri Cathedram" (June 29, 1959) and repeated with little variation on many occasions, may be summarized thus: The One True Church of which the successor of St. Peter is the shepherd, must be purified in truth, charity, and unity. It must be without spot or blemish and reinforced and made more relevant to the present age. Then one can say to those who

13

bear the name of Christian but are outside the fold: "The way is open. This is our Father's House; take or retake your place in it."

At first, Pope John said nothing to distinguish unity from union. As late as the summer of 1960 he created a secretariat to deal with union. Soon, however, it became "The Secretariat for Promoting Christian Unity." (On unity and union, see Chapter 8.) The Pope also gave the council the official designation "The Second Vatican Council." This made it clear that it was not to be confined to the unfinished business of the First Vatican Council (interrupted when the troops of Italian unification entered Rome in September, 1870, and ended the pope's rule over the papal States). It also made it easier for non-Catholics* to refer to the coming Council, since "ecumenical" is used with various meanings, as we shall see. The relation between Christian unity and church union will also be further explored.

The gap between Roman Catholics and other Christians is wide and deep. The Eastern Orthodox churches and the Roman Catholic Church have been separate since 1054. The massive separation of Protestant churches from Rome began with the sixteenth-century Reformation. The chasm was enlarged by the First Vatican Council of 1869-70, when it defined and promulgated the doctrine of papal infallibility. A major question now is whether the Second Vatican Council will reduce the

---

* To avoid monotony, Catholic with capital "C" is frequently used throughout the book for Roman Catholic. "Roman" is used without prejudice, being part of the full official name. All Christians declare themselves catholic when they recite the Apostles' Creed.

breach, as Pope John obviously desires, or widen it still further.

Additional Possibilities

The Council will also discuss and act, or refuse to act, on matters of great concern not directly related to Christian unity. Some of its actions, or failures to act where it might, will affect all mankind. Christian unity in action would, of course, greatly increase the churches' influence on peace, race relations, and other moral and social issues. United action would, in turn, further develop the churches' unity. Before turning to possibilities of Council action on moral and social issues that concern all men, however, one needs to ask in what different ways the Second Vatican Council concerns each of the three major Christian groups.

It is well to remember, while emphasizing the responsibility of Roman Catholics for the manifesting of Christian unity, that other Christians also have, and recognize, a corresponding responsibility. Far from diminishing the importance of the Council, the general and increasing concern for Christian unity makes the Council more timely, more relevant. It is, in fact, morally imperative. The movement or movements that seek to promote Christian unity throughout the world are called ecumenical. Their extent, nature, and significance will be considered later.

Why It Is Important for Roman Catholics

Why and how is the Second Vatican Council important to Roman Catholics? One good and sufficient reason is that the Pope has called for it. As indicated above, he has linked his pontificate to the Council. Pope John's conception of the Council will be further reported in subsequent chapters.

Council proceedings, added to four years of preparations, will bring home to Catholics a new sense of their Church: its size, its world-wide extent, its variety, the growing demand and capacity of clergy and laity to play a more vital role as Catholics, both in the Church and in the world.

At the same time, if they are attentive to the whole story as it unfolds, they will have a fresh, in many cases an overwhelming, sense of the interdependence of all Christians—that is, of the need for Christian unity not only in spirit but in action. There are many situations where such a realization, on their part and on that of their fellow Christians, would be no less than revolutionary. Christians might talk more *with* each other, not merely at, about, or against!

If Catholics pay attention to their fellow Christians' reactions to the Council, they will understand that their Church does not seem the same from outside as from within. They can then work more intelligently to remove manifestations and correct attitudes that have long been barriers to understanding, to co-operation, to unity of spirit. Realizing and correcting their own shortcomings, they can better help fellow Christians to realize wherein they have been unjust or offensive to Catholics or have failed to present their own true faith and character to them.

Through the Council, more Catholics will learn, as many of them already know, what it means to be a world church. Not only has it a major responsibility for

Christian unity. It can vitally affect world peace, race relations, relations with non-Christian religions, religious liberty, the relation between rich nations and poor, and the ratio of population to food supply. For Rome is now the center of a world church in a sense and to a degree almost undreamed of when the First Vatican Council met. Then, if Europe did not bound its interests it usually dominated them, especially in temporal matters.

Roman Catholics, at least in Europe and North America, are increasingly interested in the role of laymen. The Council will pay much attention to what is called the apostolate of the laity. Will the outcome be merely plans and machinery to channel lay efforts in predetermined directions? Or will laymen be in a sense emancipated, set free to use their loyal and consecrated energies in the twentieth-century world in which they live? One hears more frequently than formerly that the Church *is* the laity. Few Protestants, probably, would believe that the statement applies to Catholics to the degree that it does to leading Protestant denominations. The Council will not be fully or finally determinative in this area. Catholic laymen will exert increasing influence and be increasingly vocal, in any case. But the Council can guide and encourage, or restrict and retard.

In sum, many Catholics, clergy and laity, are hoping that the Second Vatican Council will turn its face to the future. They value to the full its wealth of tradition, of piety and charity and martyrdom. But they also feel a certain weight of inertia, self-satisfaction, even provincialism. Encouraged and challenged by Pope John's call for "aggiornamento"—bringing the church up to date, making it increasingly relevant to the life and problems

of the 1960's—they are working and praying in the hope
that the Council will respond to his call. Then, as a
Catholic publisher writes, "the Church will become, in
virtue of what She *is*, the most compelling argument and
persuasive invitation to unity."

All Christians are Involved

And why is this Council important to Christians outside the Church of Rome? That Church numbers five
hundred million members, well over half of those who
call themselves Christian. Nothing that affects them
vitally can be without importance to other Christians.

As we shall see more fully in Chapters 6 and 7, there
is wide, deep, and active concern for Christian unity
among Protestants, Anglicans, and Eastern Orthodox,
which has developed with speed and momentum during
the past fifty years. Those involved in movements growing out of that concern are necessarily thereby involved
in the outcome of Roman Catholic efforts having the
same intended or possible direction. The different forces
may clash, coalesce, or remain for a long time parallel.
The Council's actions, attitudes, and atmosphere will
count for much in determining the future.

By creating a climate favorable to the participation of
Catholics in dialogue—attentive listening and honest
speaking—across confessional lines, the announcement of
the Council has already substantially contributed, at
least temporarily, to the cause of Christian unity. An
American priest was one of fifty responding to an invitation to a conversation with Protestants soon after Pope
John's announcement. He remarked that not more than
ten or twelve would have responded before the Council

was announced. The setting up of the Secretariat for Promoting Christian Unity provides a channel, at present, for an exchange of views with representatives of non-Roman churches. Previously, such exchanges were private and unofficial, and sometimes secret. Will the Council further encourage conversations at all levels? Will it favor continuing and strengthening the Secretariat?

Must They "Return"?

Will the Council continue to maintain the Roman Catholic thesis that the price of manifesting Christian unity is the return of the "separated brethren" to the Roman Catholic Church? It is evident that all Christians must somehow return to at least as much unity as apparently existed through the first ten centuries of the Christian era. The question is whether all the "returning" has to be done by Protestants, Anglicans, and the Eastern Orthodox. The Second Vatican Council will be the twenty-first in the series which most Roman Catholics recognize as general councils of the Church. The first eight, beginning with Nicaea, 325 A.D., were held in the Near East, the rest in western Europe, but only one, 1869-70, at the Vatican. The Eastern and Western churches were united only in the first seven. The Council of Trent, 1545-63, on the heels of the Protestant Reformation, was the nineteenth.

Pope John continues to use the language of return. He has said that when the Church has purified and brought itself up to date through the Second Vatican Council it will then be possible for "separated brethren" to recognize the Roman Catholic Church as their true home and take or retake their place in it. If the Council succeeds in

carrying out the task defined for it by Pope John, will
that not in itself contribute to the possibility for all Christians to move in the direction of the more visible unity
which the Catholics now enjoy? This will be examined
more in detail in later chapters. We shall then see that in
some regards the Eastern Orthodox refusal to admit the
propriety of the word "return" is even sharper than that
of the Protestants.

Mariology

Will the Council encourage the present trend toward
the development of the cult of the Virgin Mary? The gap
here between Protestants and Roman Catholics is wider
than that between Roman Catholics and the Eastern
Orthodox. Many excellent writings by Protestants in recent years attest to their loyalty to the Virgin Mary, their
appreciation of her role as depicted in the New Testament. They fear, however, that the popular attention increasingly devoted to Mary in many areas will tend to
withdraw attention from Jesus Christ, and that the devo-
tion and veneration now paid to Mary may develop into
real worship, and into her exaltation, therefore, both in
practice and in theory, to a fully divine role. There are
many Catholics who, while not criticizing the doctrines
laid down, feel that the emphasis, especially the popular
emphasis, on Mariology, the cult of the Virgin, is tending
already to distract the minds of believers from the supe-
rior and more essential role of her divine Son. It is one
thing for Catholics themselves to go as far as their mind
and their conscience lead them in their religious practices with regard to the Virgin Mary. It is quite another
thing if they insist that all Christians must accept their

full doctrine and practice in order to achieve adequate manifestation of Christian unity.

The Bible: Bond or Barrier?

Americans of all faiths will be watching with great interest the atmosphere, attitudes, and possible action of the Second Vatican Council with regard to the Bible. There is strong Catholic and Protestant support for an English translation acceptable to both. Catholic interest in the wider ecumenical movement has been stimulated by the joint participation of Catholic and Protestant theologians in discussions of biblical questions. Cardinal Bea has been a notable leader in such discussions. How far can such joint studies be extended consistently with Catholic tradition? Will the Council encourage the notable increase during recent decades in Bible reading and the publication of fresh translations within Catholicism? Will there be a clear and strong statement regarding the authority of the Bible? There are at least five of the preparatory commissions that might well have considered such questions and made recommendations for Council discussion and action.

A little-known but well-authenticated incident from World War II days illustrates the delicacy for Catholics of such questions, and their increasing readiness to face them. A Swiss Protestant serving Italian prisoners of war in North Africa under the auspices of the World Alliance of YMCAs, unable to secure the needed number of authorized texts for the Catholic prisoners, went to Pope Pius XII with his problem. "It is difficult," said the Pontiff, "to understand the Holy Scripture without the proper commentary. But it is most important that it be available, and that it be read and pondered. Use Protestant translations if you must."

In Rome, January, 1962, it was the author's privilege to visit the Abbey of St. Jerome, where a dozen monks of high scholarship are studying, collating, and publishing texts and other documents that contribute to a "pure" Latin text of the Bible. They and temporary or part-time helpers, already at work for more than ten years and with a dozen solid volumes to their credit, hope in another fifteen years to complete their work—with some fifteen additional volumes—on the Old Testament.

In the United States, the Paulist Fathers in New York and the Benedictine monks in Collegeville, Minnesota, are putting similar scholarship into the production in English of a series of studies, suitable for groups or individuals, of books of the Bible.

Protestant Concern and Influence

As will be evident from later chapters, many Catholics are quite sensitive to Protestant voices. They will have at least an indirect influence on the Council and on Catholic thinking and action in general. The skepticism and pessimism of many Protestants with regard to the Vatican Council—and indeed, with regard to the whole Roman Catholic Church—may itself serve to some degree as a stimulus. One feels confident, however, that the more friendly and understanding challenge of Protestants who fervently desire that Christian unity shall be made manifest, and who are not entirely pessimistic with regard to the Council, will have a greater effect.

More General Concerns

Questions so far listed as being of concern to Roman Catholics and Protestants are not confined to those groups for their results or interests, but they do involve church doctrines and practices. There are other questions of interest to men in general, as citizens and as human beings, which do not have such distinctly religious elements or overtones, but may nonetheless be resolved largely through the influence of the churches.

Scientism and Atheism

One such area of concern is the relation between science and religion. Here we are confronted, not so much by the old struggles connected with the names of Galileo or Darwin, but with the climate which seems to envelop the world. This is the climate of trust in science and its ability to solve all our problems and supply all our needs. There still remain, of course, old questions of interpretation—of the accommodation of a scientific attitude and a religious attitude so that each may supplement, correct, and enrich the other. There are, however, at least two quite fundamental questions. Is there any vital truth which comes to man by what we call revelation which is not to be had through science? Are men capable of supplying all their needs, solving all their problems with their own energies and devices? Christians have, and must have, convictions on these matters, and the Council can be of great help in clarifying the issues and reaffirming the Christian faith in terms and applications relevant to the twentieth century, if it responds adequately to Pope John's appeals.

When scientism and overconfidence in science are

joined to atheism, the problem is no longer in the field of possible compromise. The churches must not only understand but must fight an atheistic materialism. The question remains, however, as to the climate in which this battle is fought, the means which are used to oppose the enemy of religion, and the care which is taken not to encourage other foes of the Church and of mankind who may be just as hostile and as dangerous to our dearest values as are the Communists. Of course, the Church must fight communism. Equally, of course, a wider and deeper and more effective Christian unity will strengthen the battle against an atheistic and tyrannical communism. Some Catholic leaders, however, have expressed the hope that Christian unity will not be presented primarily as a device to fight a political battle. They hope that the Council will not be, and will not be considered, chiefly as a kind of crusade against communism. Thoughtful Catholics are becoming increasingly aware of the political and religious danger of allowing dictators of the right to count upon an unenlightened support from large Catholic populations. It is not likely, nor do they think it necessary, that the Council should lay down a political ideology. It will have a beneficial effect on society if, by its actions and by its attitudes, it supports the trends progressively developed in the three encyclicals of 1891, 1931, and 1961—known respectively as "Rerum Novarum," "Quadragesimo Anno," and "Mater et Magistra" (from the opening words of the Latin texts)—which together form a foundation for the rights and dignity of working men, and their protection by society in the interest of society as a whole.

World Peace

Few would assert that any of the world's religions have yet found a way to deal adequately with the overwhelming problem of world peace. All have contributed and are contributing to its solution. The Roman Catholic Church, existing throughout the world, with exceptional opportunities for teaching and persuading, bears a large responsibility for the avoidance of war and the building of a true and just peace for all men. Many Catholics are hoping that the coming Council will find a way to deal effectively, or at least very helpfully, with this problem, in line with statements and actions by Pope John.

Some Catholics would consider it opportune to review and revise the whole doctrine of the "just war." Responsible churchmen, even when they can rise above purely national considerations, hesitate to say or do anything that seems to take away from the natural right of self-defense. It is a fair question today, however, to ask just how much right of self-defense is enjoyed by nine-tenths of the nations of the world and more than 99 per cent of the population of the world. The Council cannot escape the challenge to emphasize both the elementary human values and the transcendent values in ways that will take account of humanity's thirst for peace and forward the search for the way to peace.

2. Possible Influences
of the Council

Having considered some possible religious and ecclesiastical impacts of the Second Vatican Council, we now turn to its possible influence on society, with considerable attention to areas of tension in the United States. But no sharp separation is attempted, or desirable, between the effects on religion and those on society, or between American and world concerns.

Furthermore, it must be borne in mind that the Council is not a provincial assembly, legislating or otherwise acting on specific local problems. Its influence on them will more likely be felt through its general orientation and the climate it helps to create with regard to interconfessional dialogue in a pluralistic society, to decentralization of authority and administration, and to the responsibility and freedom of laymen. Its influence may consist of recognizing the world of the twentieth century, as several recent popes have sometimes sought to lead their Church to do, or of clinging to medieval forms and substance, as has often seemed to be the preference of the Curia and of the semi-official "Osservatore Romano."

Education

It is in the field of primary and secondary education that the questions of church-state relations, religious liberty, and Protestant-Catholic relations seem to produce the most and the deepest tensions in the United States. Among the questions are: tax support, direct or indirect, for the benefit of parochial schools; such fringe benefits as bus transportation, luncheon, and textbooks; religion in the curriculum; the observance of religious holidays; and approval or disapproval of bond issues for the support of public education. On some of these matters Protestants and Catholics are nearer to each other than they are to the Jews. On some, the division is between the secular community and the religious community as a whole. While the Council will not as a rule deal with local or provincial problems as such, it might help on these, as in other areas, by facilitating a climate of calm discussion, rather than one of acute and sometimes stormy controversy. It might also, either by specific action or by its general orientation, aid in answering two of the questions that become involved in these educational controversies: Does the Roman Catholic Church insist on controlling the whole curriculum of each Catholic child as a matter both of right and of policy? How far does the Church recognize the civil rights of the non-religious taxpayer, and consequently the need to consider his interest in deciding religious questions that relate to the public school and its curriculum?

Decentralization and Local Matters

Other problems than those in the field of education which are of interest to Americans would be affected by an increase in the authority of the bishop, as part of the process of decentralization. A number of American Catholics wonder why it is necessary that many decisions on marriage and divorce be referred to Rome. They feel that this not only clogs the administrative channels in Rome unduly but also causes undue delay in the settlement of questions which, after all, are to be decided upon generally recognized and well-defined principles of Roman Catholicism, the only variant being the judgment of the hierarchy. The bishop, they feel, being so much nearer to the given case is in a better position than anyone in Rome to decide how to apply Catholic principles to the given case.

Decentralization is in line, it would seem, with the general principle of subsidiarity expressed by Pope Pius XII and appealed to with increasing frequency by Catholics. This means, roughly, that social problems are to be dealt with as far as possible by the group nearest the problem, in the ascending order of competence. This would seem to have relevance, for example, to Catholic membership in a Rotary Club or a Christian Association (YMCA, YWCA). Catholic principles are universal—the policy is uniform—but the application may vary with conditions from one locality to another.

With regard to the Christian Associations, there is at least the beginning of a recognition among Catholics, including Vatican circles, of the part that the "Y's" have played and can play in the ecumenical movement. It seems likely, therefore, that there will be less and less objection to participation in the cultural and recreational and physical activities of the Associations. There are areas where Catholics are ready to participate also in their religious activities. It is not easy, however, to devise "religious activities" which appeal equally to Catholics and Protestants and in which they can therefore participate together. Promising experiments are being conducted, and Catholics, Orthodox, and Protestants realize increasingly that if the Associations are to make their potential contribution to the wider ecumenical movement, more and better solutions must be found. This would seem to be rather obviously an area in which the bishop, being nearer to the experiment, can better judge its value. The YMCA has had working agreements with Orthodox authorities through several decades. There would seem to be no reason why the Vatican Council should make either specific or general pronouncements in this matter. If, however, it underscores and defines the authority of the bishop, leaving him the necessary freedom, and if the total climate of the Council encourages such experiments, then lay Christian organizations, including membership from the three major groupings, can make a great contribution to the total ecumenical movement.

Church-State Co-operation

In the field of church-state relations, perhaps the chief question in the minds of Americans, both Protestant and Catholic, is how far the Council and the Roman Catholic Church as a whole will take note of and profit by the nearly unique experience in the United States. This seems to demonstrate adequately that the government and religious bodies can co-operate with mutual profit, without infringing upon the rights of conscience or the interests of one particular church. Thus a very strong and influential section of Roman Catholicism has learned that the Church does not need the support of the state, nor does it need to control the state. The proximate question would seem to be, therefore, not whether the Roman Catholic Church will make great efforts to dominate politics and government in North America, but whether it will be encouraged by the North American and other experiences to become less dependent upon governments in other countries, particularly Latin ones, and correspondingly feel less need to control those governments. Many Catholics in America and elsewhere would say that this is not a question of revising doctrine, but one of facing the circumstances attendant upon the religious pluralism which is the present fact in many countries and seems certain to spread and be encountered more widely. The national secretary of Catholic Action in Canada said, in the summer of 1961, that Quebec's Catholics are "honestly seeking ways of development for the Province that will neither offend the principles and rights of the Church nor infringe upon the legitimate claims of government." He called for a more mature attitude on church-state relations, and emphasized both the concern and the competence of laymen in this field.

The Lay Apostolate

Catholic laymen in North America seem to be increasingly concerned and competent, both in the religious apostolate, as such, and in the application of Roman Catholic doctrine, tradition, and spirit to civic problems. Thus the Commission for the Apostolate of the Laity attracts the interest and the hopes of many Catholic laymen. (For commissions, see Chapters 3 and 5.)

Free and active participation of Catholic laymen in expressing a Catholic viewpoint in community controversies or conversation would seem to be a prime necessity in American life, both religiously and politically. What the Commission suggests, and what the Council does, in this field is therefore of great concern to both Catholic and Protestant Americans. Thoughtful Catholic laymen already active in this sense are convinced that their free participation will not only continue but even increase. This involves no desire or necessity to modify Catholic doctrine. It is a part of what is implied by Pope John's demand that the Church be brought up to date in its relation to the culture and the problems of mankind. Americans working with this Commission as members or consultants are: Bishop Allen James Babcock of Grand Rapids; Bishop Fulton J. Sheen of New York; Msgr. George Higgins of the National Catholic Welfare Conference, Washington, D. C.; and Msgr. Luigi Ligutti of Iowa, who is papal observer to the Food and Agriculture Organization. There have been successful attempts by the Catholic press of the United States to draw out and express the interest of laymen with regard to the Council.

Laymen have a necessary and very important double role to play in manifesting Christian unity. Their readiness for it and their desire for it will stimulate both theologians and bishops. And however much is achieved at the theological level and at the Council level, Christian unity cannot become visible to the world as a whole and to the local community until it is realized by and among laymen of all confessions. Thus Bishop John J. Wright of Pittsburgh has declared that it is no longer heresy which divides the Christian churches as much as the by-products of culture, of memories of the clash of common institutions. He stresses that the way of reunion, for a long time to come, must be prepared by the broadening of individual attitudes. Bishop Wright is a member of the Theological Commission for the Second Vatican Council. His statement clearly implies the part which laymen must play in bringing about Christian unity. Catholic bishops, theologians, and editors are devoting increasing attention to the role of the laity. The Council faces here an important and impressive challenge and opportunity.

On this subject, Fr. Robert A. Graham, S.J., of *America*, the national Jesuit weekly, has written that, "while the zeal of the first Christians brought Christ's gospel to the limits of the Roman empire, it may be this age's privilege to extend that kingdom in a great leap forward to the ends of the earth." "It remains only for the fathers of the Council to give formal recognition," Father Graham continues, "to the lay apostolic movement, which has been sweeping the Church for many years." Father Graham buttresses his emphatic affirmation with quotations from Pope John XXIII and references to what the Central Commission has said and proposes. Father Graham would hope that the Second Vatican Council might even earn the name "Council of the Lay Apostolate."

Race Relations

Will the Council find a way to encourage and support those who are striving to bring about better race relations? A Catholic editor, an American widely known and influential in the wider ecumenical movement, has expressed the hope "that the Council would condemn in explicit terms all forms of racism as a denial of the universality of redemption, and all forms of racial discrimination as affronts to human dignity." The editor coupled this hope with the related one "that, since human rights are rooted in—indeed, derive from—the natural law, the Council should declare that civil rights should not be conditioned by confessional allegiance."

The doctrines are doubtless clear enough. But they must not be widely enough known when Catholic laymen in Louisiana attempt to appeal over the Archbishop's head to the Pope, asking support for a policy of racial discrimination. The problem, of course, is not confined to the Catholic Church. Protestant laymen and clergymen sometimes find it possible to dispute what most churches hold to be the clear teachings of the Bible with regard to the brotherhood of all men.

Pope Benedict XV, soon after World War I, gave great impetus to making his Church a world church through recognizing and promoting an indigenous clergy in lands outside the Christian culture. There are now a great many non-white prelates, who will be members of the Council, from Asian and African nations.

Religious Liberty

Most non-Catholics, and many Catholics, are very much interested in the whole problem of religious liberty. This problem has many aspects. It affects church-state relations, and principles of religious liberty are invoked by both parties in the struggle between parochial and public schools for tax money. Religious liberty is involved to some extent in the problems attendant upon mixed marriages, the practice of non-Catholic physicians in Catholic hospitals, adoptions, sectarian content in the public school curriculum, credit for courses in religion, and the observance of religious holidays.

It can be confidently affirmed that the Second Vatican Council will not greatly advance the cause of Christian unity unless it contributes to the support of religious liberty. The converse is not necessarily true, as a general proposition. Protestants for centuries practiced more and more liberty with less and less manifest unity. But while doctrinal freedom with its resulting divergence has given rise to many denominations, it has contributed to the development of free speech and has put religious liberty under the legal protection of the state. For many decades now, the confusion of tongues among major Protestant bodies has been decreasing. More and more their essential unity is seen and felt. Their total experience, far from putting liberty in opposition to unity, shows that no real unity can be achieved under coercion, whether by state or Church.

Concordats in Latin America

Protestant-Catholic relations in the United States are involved in some foreign problems and episodes as well as in various domestic ones. Religious tensions in the Republic of Colombia are a case in point. These, and similar ones in other predominantly Catholic nations, may well be affected by Council action. Colombia is one of the few countries in the Western Hemisphere that have a concordat with the Vatican, a special sort of treaty that gives the Roman Catholic Church certain legal rights and privileges not enjoyed by other religious bodies. How is a concordat to be construed when a country adopts a constitution, or wishes to do so, that is not fully compatible with the concordat's provisions? How does the concordat affect previous or subsequent treaties with a power that insists on religious liberty for its nationals, resident in the Catholic country, and grants it to those of the Catholic faith resident in the non-Catholic country? Such questions have contributed to the delay or prevention of the ratification or renewal of treaties between the United States and two Latin American countries, Colombia and Haiti, during the past decade. Such reports as those from Colombia—and Spain—have adversely affected the attitude of many Protestants towards the Roman Catholic Church as a whole.

Tensions in the United States

It is also important to look at the effect which the difficulties in Colombia have had on Protestant-Catholic relations in the United States. Conflicting reports from Colombia have appeared in the Protestant and Catholic presses of the United States, and sometimes in the secular press. Leaders in the United States from both confessions, working together, have tried to get at both the facts of the incidents reported from Colombia and the underlying sociological, historical, and religious bases of the incidents. This co-operative effort has been useful in itself as far as the United States is concerned. The address of Pope Pius XII to Catholic jurists in Italy in December, 1953, has been used to good effect by both Protestants and Catholics. He said in effect that tolerance would be required for the sake of good relations with nations where Roman Catholics are not the majority or dominant group. Since the end of the dictatorship in Colombia, conditions have improved. But who knows when they will worsen there or in some other country? What the Second Vatican Council does to improve the general ecumenical climate, to support the Christian conscience in its inherent rights, and to show that Pope Pius' directive is really accepted, may have a powerful effect on such situations.

Anti-Semitism

Whether in dealing with religion and education, with race relations, or with religious liberty, the Council has the opportunity, and has been invited by Jews and Christians, to throw its weight against anti-Semitism. Pope John's elimination from the ritual of the word "infidels," referring to Jews, set a minor but significant example for his Church. In following it, will the Council, while avoiding any theological syncretism or nationalistic involvements, perhaps find ways to reduce the specifically "Christian" prejudices which still account for much anti-Jewish sentiment and discrimination?

Population and Food

Another point at which difficulty arises is the world problem of establishing a livable relation between the population level and the food supply. The lack of this is an impediment to world peace, and tempts hungry people to accept the apparent shortcut of communism. There is general agreement that the food supply of the world can be vastly increased. Many would agree that, once a proper ratio were established, it could be maintained for a very long time in the future. A practical difficulty is that no such ratio has ever been achieved. We do not start from a proper starting point. The union of Catholic and non-Catholic efforts is highly desirable, perhaps absolutely necessary, if we are ever to achieve a tolerable condition with regard to the relation of population to the food supply. How farseeing, how realistic, how imaginative can one hope that the Council will be in dealing with this problem? Will it recognize that there is a problem? Many Roman Catholics do, and take it seriously. Will the Council contribute to the discussion of sharp and vital differences in this area in a climate of mutual tolerance?

It is in connection with this problem that controversy arises with regard to planned parenthood. Roman Catholics have a right to their convictions and practices. They also have a right, and from their point of view may even have a duty, to try to persuade others to share their convictions and follow their practices. But many citizens, of all faiths and of none, object to any effort through government forces to impose these practices upon others, either Christian or non-Christian. There seems to be, at least in the United States, increasing agreement and understanding between Roman Catholics and non-Catholics that education and religion may, within the control of the respective faith bodies, do all that is possible to carry out the convictions of each religious body and to witness to its faith before outsiders, but that government channels are not to be used for such ends.

Catholic Trade Unions

Many Americans, independently of their creeds, would be greatly disturbed if the Council should try to tip the scales in favor of Catholic trade unions. They have been encouraged in some countries in the fight against communism. The 1961 encyclical "Mater et Magistra" seems not to have encouraged their formation where they do not exist. Will the Council leave such matters to local and area decision? Since collective bargaining seems to be fully accepted by the encyclical, a good question would seem to be whether the Council, by some specific reference, might help to make it a reality in a few countries, predominantly Catholic, where a dictatorship of the right exists. This would gratify many American union leaders and members, Catholic and non-Catholic; it would strengthen the West as a whole in its struggle with the dictatorships of the left, which are, by their ideology, not amenable to a direct religious appeal.

No Holy War?

How will the Council contribute to the struggle against communism? Catholic and other voices have been raised to express the hope that the Council will not become primarily an instrument in the cold war, or encourage the idea of a holy war against atheistic materialism. But it may well aid in the struggle, they would say, by all that it does: for Christian unity; for the recognition of the individual's worth and dignity, and the inviolability of his conscience; for the conscientious acceptance by rich individuals and nations of their duty toward the less privileged; and for the support of the United Nations and world peace. Pope John has not been derelict in these matters; the Council may find ways to strengthen his hands.

Religion and Politics

Implicit in some of these questions are the more general ones of the extent and the manner of church participation in political controversy, domestic and international. Mr. Martin Work, executive director of the National Council of Catholic Men, said in October, 1960, "We don't want the Church in politics . . . we don't want the Church involved in the work of the state. . . . Nor do we want the state intruding into church affairs." In Italy, many Catholics would say "amen" to this most heartily, but would agree that their Church has not always lived up to the principle and would express regret at the language and apparent meaning of the "Fixed Points" mentioned in Chapter 5. In Germany a few years ago, an archbishop undertook privately to reprove a Catholic who ran for Parliament to represent another party than Adenauer's. The candidate, on grounds of Catholic doctrine, rejected the reproof and was elected. Whether the Council will think it advisable to guard against possible bad effects of the "Fixed Points" is, of course, a delicate question, but it might be of great service in the future to those—Catholics, Protestants, and Jews—in the United States who sought in 1960 to show that the election of a Catholic to the presidency ought not to become the occasion of an interfaith or interconfessional battle.

A Protestant leader with long experience on three continents wrote, for a survey for Religious News Service made by the author: "It's too much to hope for, but *I'd like to see* the Pope pull his Church completely out of power politics on all levels, parochial, national, and international." Many who would like to agree with this would hesitate both on semantic and substantive grounds to commit themselves to every word. For example, is it power politics to rebuke a dictator in Russia or China or Cuba? Or Spain or Portugal? Should the Vatican cease

to accept ambassadors from those nations that want to
send them? Again, it is to the Council's climate and general attitudes, almost certainly, rather than to specific
declarations, that one must look for its influence on the
Church's political habits.

3. The Council
and How It Works

The Second Vatican Council is recognized by most Roman Catholics as the twenty-first General Council of their Church. It is commonly and officially termed an ecumenical council. However, the Eastern Orthodox consider that only the first seven general councils were ecumenical. It seems that no council has put forth a clear definition of what is required in order that a council may be called ecumenical.

"Catholic" and "Ecumenical"

The terms "ecumenical" and "catholic" are practically interchangeable; each means universal. But clearly, what Catholics regard as universal is not necessarily what is regarded as universal by the other two major Christian groupings, the Eastern Orthodox and the Protestants.*

When Pope John announced, a few months after the first proclamation of a general council, that it was to be called the Second Vatican Council, he made it easier for non-Roman Catholics to refer to the Council without

---

* For convenience, "Protestant" is used to refer to trinitarian communions that are neither Eastern Orthodox nor Roman Catholic. Among the larger communions, difficulty in accepting the Protestant label is encountered, notably among the Anglicans. (Among Southern Baptists, some maintain that they are not Protestants.)

having to call it "ecumenical," contrary to their own convictions.

One should note the double use of the term "the ecumenical movement." It is often used of the movement of which the World Council of Churches is a manifestation. More will be said of the World Council of Churches in Chapter 6. But writers of all confessions often refer to "the ecumenical movement" as the total movement or sum of movements which have as their goal the clearer manifestation of Christian unity. In this sense, it seems convenient to refer to the wider or the total ecumenical movement.

The Pope Can Govern without a Council

One may well ask how the Roman Catholic Church can manage, holding councils as infrequently as it does. The Council of Trent, nineteenth in the series, was held in the middle of the sixteenth century, just over 400 years ago. Three centuries then elapsed before the First Vatican Council assembled, and it has now been almost a century since it met. An adequate answer to our question would involve a rather full history of the Roman Catholic Church and a rather complete description of its structure. For our purpose let us say, first, that the council is not a parliament. Its acts are not binding unless and until they are approved by the pope. The pope, on the other hand, has adequate authority without the support of a council. During most of the fifteenth century, a struggle for supremacy went on between partisans of pope and council. This was settled in favor of the pope by the time of the Council of Trent. The First Vatican Council, in an action desired and approved by Pope Pius

IX, promulgated the doctrine of papal infallibility. When the pope makes it plain that he is speaking *ex cathedra,* that is, with full and declared papal authority, he is speaking with the full authority of the Church, and his words are binding on all Roman Catholics. When the pope does not speak *ex cathedra,* his teaching is nevertheless considered as authoritative. He occasionally writes general letters—encyclicals—to the Church. During the pontificate of Pius XII there was an apparent advance in the binding character of the papal messages. For example, his address to Italian Catholic jurists in December, 1953, in the field of religious liberty is to be generally accepted as papal teaching and binding on all Catholics, according to assurances given the author in Rome by both progressive and conservative spokesmen.

Not only does the pope have sufficient authority to rule without a council; he has an elaborate administrative organization. For each of the major concerns of the Church there is a congregation, headed by a cardinal, with an adequate staff. The Sacred Congregation of the Holy Office, for example, deals with matters of doctrine. It has all the authority today which it had when it was commonly called the Inquisition. To other congregations are entrusted the propagation of the faith, worship, discipline, matters related to the Oriental churches, and other matters mainly internal. There is also a secretariat dealing with matters of state. These various bodies are collectively referred to as the "Curia," which means court in the old monarchial sense. Their members and staff resident in Rome number in the hundreds.

It is not even necessary for the pope to assemble a council in order to have the advice of the bishops around the world. A very careful sort of referendum preceded the proclamation of the dogma of the assumption of the Virgin Mary. Also, bishops have their appointed schedule of regular visits to Rome and to the pope, called *ad limina* (to the threshold).

Why Was the Second Vatican Council Called?

Since it is evident that the Pope could have continued to go forward without a general council, it is proper to ask, why did he in fact announce the Second Vatican Council? Until Christmas, 1961, the Council had only been announced, not summoned. The general tenor of the Pope's messages concerning the Council in the thirty-five months between announcement and convocation was indicated at the beginning of Chapter 1. It is appropriate to note, at this point, his concerns as reflected in these excerpts from the bull (formal papal document bearing the *bulla*, or seal) by which he announced the Second Vatican Council for 1962 (the exact date, October 11, was announced only on February 2):

> The forthcoming Council will meet, therefore, and at a moment in which the Church finds very alive the desire to fortify its Faith and to contemplate itself in its own awe-inspiring unity. In the same way it feels more urgent the duty to give greater efficiency to its sound vitality and to promote the sanctification of its members, the diffusion of revealed truth, the consolidation of its agencies.

Among internal matters requiring "greater efficiency" and what Pope John elsewhere styled "aggiornamento"— bringing up to date—Catholics have spoken or written of the role of bishops, other clergy, the laity, the orders, the use of the vernacular in most of the worship, and revival of the permanent diaconate.

The external circumstances demanding attention, viz., divisions among Christians, and a confused and threatened world, are indicated in these two additional paragraphs from the Christmas Day Bull:

> Then, at a time of generous and growing efforts which are made in different parts for the purpose of rebuilding that visible unity of all Christians which corresponds to the wishes of the Divine Redeemer, it is very natural that the forthcoming Council should provide premises of doctrinal clarity and of mutual charity that will make still more alive in our separated brethren the wish for the hoped-for return to unity and will smooth the way. . . .
>
> And finally, to a world which is lost, confused, and anxious under the constant threat of new, frightful conflicts, the forthcoming Council must offer a possibility for all men of good will to turn their thoughts and their intentions toward peace, a peace which can and must, above all, come from spiritual and supernatural realities, from human intelligence and conscience, enlightened and guided by God the Creator and Redeemer of humanity.

Popes Pius XI and Pius XII, according to Catholic writers, had seen the need for a council, but had not found a period sufficiently free from crisis and the atmosphere of crisis to make a definite decision to that effect. Meanwhile, the "generous and growing efforts" for unity inside, and particularly outside, the Church of Rome had been growing rapidly. While it would be hazardous, though not without plausibility, to suggest, as some observers have done, that the development of the World Council of Churches was a factor in persuading

Pope John to announce the Vatican Council, its existence and importance do contribute to the timeliness of the Pope's decision. As a subsequent chapter will make clear, the World Council of Churches represents Christian forces parallel to those of Rome, which must be taken into account where Christian unity and the Christian impact on society are under consideration.

Membership and Meetings

Granted the need for the Council, one wants to know a number of things concerning its constitution, preparation, and operation. All bishops and heads of large religious orders will be members of the Council. This includes the titular bishops, those who do not actually administer a diocese. It does not include the lower clergy or laymen. The number of official members will be in the neighborhood of three thousand, as compared with about seven hundred in the First Vatican Council.

The Council will meet in Christendom's largest church edifice—St. Peter's. The First Vatican Council also met in a section of this church. Many Catholics are hopeful that there will be a minimum of pomp and ceremony connected with this Council. They would agree, however, that there must be certain public occasions. These will, of course, provide a magnificent spectacle for all the world to see.

Councils have varied in duration. The Council of Trent, for example, met in 1545 and, with some intervals, continued to meet until 1563. With present travel facilities, the Council is likely to recess after two months (mid-October to mid-December) and resume its work for another two months between New Year's and Easter, or between Easter and the short Roman summer, 1963. In April, 1962, the author was informed that the bishops would receive the *schema*—the material to be considered by the Council—not earlier than July. One consequence of the brevity of the period remaining for study might be the postponement of some of the more difficult questions until the second session.

The official language of the Council and all its preparatory bodies is Latin. It was announced early that there would not be the system of simultaneous translation used in large international secular assemblies. It is probable that a few bishops, particularly from Asia and Africa, will not have a ready command of the Latin language. Necessary concessions will be made for them. A special secretariat has been created to give out Council news both during the preparatory period and during the assembly itself. It will make its releases available as rapidly as possible in several languages.

Catholic Constituency Consultation

The first stage of the Council's work was designated as ante-preparatory. This period lasted some eighteen months. During that time, bishops and heads of seminaries around the world consulted their fellow Catholics and sent in their opinions and desires with regard to the Council. That material was assembled and collated in fifteen volumes totaling more than nine thousand pages. The first volume, the only one made public, contains the Pope's speeches that refer to the Council up to the summer of 1960. The rest is secret as far as the public is concerned, but was classified and indexed for the convenience of the various bodies engaged in preparing the work of the Council.

Why the secrecy? If these official matters were published indiscriminately, they would not be simultaneously known or uniformly understood by members of the Council. Premature discussion of the question of papal infallibility interfered greatly with its serious discussion in the First Vatican Council. The press also learned of invitations that were sent to Eastern Orthodox leaders, inviting them to attend the Council. When the leaders received these invitations they returned them unopened, saying that since they had read them in the press it was unnecessary to open them. Thoughtful Catholics give a more positive reason for secrecy: those engaged in preparation for the Council have the need and the right to go about their task in privacy and with prayerful meditation.

We should not exaggerate the negative effect of this formal secrecy. It has been possible to learn a great deal about the probable orientation of the Council from speeches and statements by the Pope, by cardinals, by theologians, and by persons engaged as staff, members, or consultants in the preparatory commissions. When a theologian describes a course that he is teaching and hands you a long article that he has written, he has given you a good idea of what he will stand for in the commission of which he is a member.

The Preparatory Bodies

Early in June, 1960, Pope John announced the formation of ten commissions besides a Central Commission, a Secretariat for Promoting Christian Unity, and two other secretariats to deal with administrative details. The ten commissions have dealt with theology, the episcopacy, church discipline, the religious orders, the sacraments, the Sacred Liturgy, studies and seminaries, the Oriental churches, missions, and the apostolate of the laity. The first, and unofficial, list did not include the laity, but that commission had been decided upon by the time the official list was published a few days later. Also, an eleventh commission was added during the summer of 1960, to deal with ceremonies, protocol, and related matters.

Each commission and secretariat is presided over by a cardinal, except the Central Commission, which is presided over by Pope John himself, and the Secretariat for Communications Media, of which an American, Archbishop Martin O'Connor, head of the North American College in Rome, is the president. In nearly every case, the cardinal who heads a commission also heads the corresponding congregation, the permanent administrative group in the Curia. Each of the preparatory bodies, organized according to its particular needs and materials, has held several plenary sessions during the two years of preparation, bringing in members and consultants from all over the world. Their work was passed on, in turn, to the Central Commission, which organized the material for communication in advance to members of the assembly and thus, in effect, prepared the agenda. The Central Commission, working under the presidency of the Pope, had also to deal with certain general questions, for instance, the matter of observers, the date, language, etc., of the Council. Additional information concerning the work of the preparatory bodies will be supplied in later chapters.

Non-Roman Observers

The question of whether there would be official observers from the other Christian confessions at the regular sessions of the Council has presented considerable difficulty. There was first the internal problem. Roman Catholic theologians who attend the Council as advisers to the bishops are not members of the Council. This makes it difficult to give status to alien observers, though conceivably both might be present at plenary meetings as listeners. But there was an even greater difficulty. The Eastern Orthodox and Roman Catholic churches have been separate since the eleventh century, when the "great schism" occurred. Each considers that it is not schismatic. Some Eastern Orthodox pointed out, as a consequence, that they could not possibly come as observers to an *ecumenical* Council, but would have to come as of right and as full members if they came at all. (See further, Professor Nissiotis' New Delhi statement, Chapter 7.)

But there is a widespread and deep concern for finding a way to acquaint non-Catholics with the true character and substance of Council discussions—a concern in which many conspicuous leaders of the major Christian groupings share. This could not be an exclusively one-way process; that is, it would involve active as well as passive participation. By June, 1962, it had been announced that representatives of other Christian communities would be invited and would be called delegate-observers. Also, conversations were being held between Monsignor Willebrands and representatives of the chief families of churches not professing allegiance to Pope John. Some of them had already indicated their intention to send representatives if invited.

4. Catholics and the Council

Pope John has spoken frequently about the Council, always in glowing terms, but usually in rather general ones. One can see in Chapters 4 and 5 what has been made of his words by those who, on the one hand, would render contemporary and relevant both the work and the image of the Church, and those who, on the contrary, are suspicious of every change. Some of the Pope's words are of encouragement to the one group; others, to the other. Inasmuch as the term "modernism" has become an opprobrious one in the Roman Catholic Church since the early days of this century, one may perhaps without impropriety or unfairness think of the two groups as the developmental and the traditional, or those who stand respectively for renewal and for restoration.

Improved Climate

An interesting contrast may be noted between the First Vatican Council and the Second Vatican Council. A hundred years ago it was, on the whole, the conservatives who wanted a council—that is, they wanted a more rigid definition of papal authority. And Pope Pius IX was quite definitely the leader of this party within the Church. It is said that he wanted to go even further than the Council finally went. Now the climate is favorable to those who believe in the need and possibility of adjustment, development, decentralization, and capitalizing the laity (whom Pius IX had to defend). Pope John, by calling the Council and by emphasizing the need for Christian unity, has opened the way for fruitful discussion. But it can scarcely be said that there is a party or that he is heading a party committed to specific measures or to a tendency within the Church that could be characterized by a single term or formula.

Pope John's Emphases

The record of some sixty speeches made by Pope John on various occasions during the two years following the announcement of the Council is available. The most frequently recurring reference in connection with the Vatican Council is to Christian unity or to the separated brethren, or to both. Almost as frequently, the Pope referred to the necessary renewal of the Church in order to make way for Christian unity. Very frequently he has included both references in a single speech. He has made it clear that only confusion would result if a direct attempt at union were made before the ground had been prepared. He has refused to prognosticate, on the ground both that the Council must be free and that it is the Holy Spirit who will guide. The Pope's favorite words have been "renewal," "reinvigorating," "purification," and bringing up to date ("aggiornamento"). But these words may mean quite different things to those, on the one hand, who still cling to the Middle Ages, and to those others who are striving to make their Church meaningful, relevant, and existential in the twentieth century.

Those who fear innovation, however, may find specific reassurance in some of the Pope's words. He has constantly spoken of the one, true Church, of the supreme pontiff as the vicar of Christ, and of the return of "separated brethren" to their true home. He has spoken with marked satisfaction of the Rome Synod of 1960. He appeals frequently to the Virgin Mary on behalf of the Council, and has also put the Council under the protection of St. Joseph.

A Pastoral Emphasis

It should be noted that Pope John is approaching the Council principally from the point of view of the good shepherd of his flock. The Council is expected to be more pastoral than doctrinal. The Pope has said that he regards the coming Council as more like the Council of Trent than like the First Vatican Council (the latter is known, of course, for its definition of papal infallibility). It is perhaps on pastoral grounds, again, that the Pope could express as much satisfaction as he has done with the Rome Synod of 1960. The Synod took note of the needs of parish priests, including erring ones, in a sympathetic way.

The Rome Synod and the "Fixed Points"

The pope is actually the bishop of Rome, one diocese of the vast Church of which he is the supreme pontiff. While the Rome Synod's actions were intended for the needs of one diocese, the prominence of the pope's own bishopric and the timing of the 1960 Synod (the first for that diocese alone!) make it significant for those interested in the Vatican Council. While much of the Synod's action was constructive, particularly in its pastoral aspects, a *Commonweal* editorial (March 4, 1960) noted some questions asked even by sympathetic non-Catholic critics:

What does it mean, they ask, when Catholics are urged
to oppose the passing of laws and regulations that injure
the Catholic faith? When the clergy are warned to give
obedience to the head of the state and secular authorities?
When Catholics are warned against reading works of Protestant, modernist, atheistic, or materialistic outlook?

Some few of the restrictive synodal principles, even as
they apply only to present-day Rome, will seem to many
too redolent of the defensive attitude adopted by the
Church in the nineteenth century. They would seem to in-
vite defensive retreat rather than positive engagement. But
this is only an additional reason why they should not be
transposed to America . . . as serious church-state or Catholic-Protestant questions.

Similarly restrictive, in the eyes of many Catholics as
well as Protestants, were the "Fixed Points." "Punti
Fermi" (Firm or Fixed Points) is the title of an article
appearing the middle of May, 1960, in the semi-official
Vatican organ "Osservatore Romano." The article was
considered quite authoritative. It asserted that the bishops have the "duty and right to guide, direct, and correct" the faithful in the political field. "It is absurd to
split the conscience into one part which is that of the
believer and one which is that of the citizen, as if the
Catholic religion were just one part of the life of the
spirit and not a central idea which orients a man's whole
existence," "Osservatore" declared.

The article stated that the hierarchy "alone has the
right to judge whether, in a certain political and social
situation, the higher principles of religious and moral
order are involved and compromised."

"A Catholic can never prescind from the teachings and
directives of the Church. In every sector of his activity

he must inspire his public and private conduct by the laws, orientations, and instructions of the hierarchy."

These do not necessarily forecast similar action by the Second Vatican Council. But they do suggest one of the major problems of Roman Catholicism. Some Catholics could not refrain from private expressions of utter dismay on first hearing of the "Punti Fermi." Asked whether the Synod could be regarded as an index to Council action, one priest replied, "Heaven forbid!" The internal problem is what physicists sometimes call a resolution of forces. Here we have, on one hand, forces arising from tradition, typified in the Latins—particularly Italian and Spanish—who seemingly dominate the congregations that make up the permanent administrative organism, the Curia. It is difficult for them to avoid a persistent nostalgia for the comfortable pre-Reformation days. With so much ecclesiastical power in their hands and so much history, doctrine, and momentum on their side, it is easy for them to feel that they alone represent the authentic Church. Some Italian Protestants are quite sure that this group has Council preparations under control, and that nothing will happen of which they disapprove. One needs to read the sometimes surprisingly conservative words of those who are known to favor coming out of the medieval atmosphere, in the light of the tremendous power and influence of this governing group.

It is not suggested that every member of this group is at every point determined to resist every sort of "aggiornamento" (bringing up to date). Also, there are more perplexing problems, the solution of which is not indicated by a mere reference to the medieval and the contemporary. One is not referring primarily to persons or to identifiable parties, but rather to tendencies, to preferred orientations for their Church. In any case, it is not easy to identify and to include in one classification those who seek to make the Roman Catholic Church more contemporary, less provincial, more ecumenical, less reliant on the exercise of temporal power, more responsive to the laity. Many persons who represent one or more of these desires have been working with intelligence and dedication in the commissions and in the Secretariat for Promoting Christian Unity. How far their influence extends into the Council, how far its members are contemporary in the senses indicated—how far, that is, the Council will truly reflect the expressed desire of Pope John—is obviously a major question. We do well to remember that this desire is, in the minds of the most existential Roman Catholics, entirely compatible with, and governed by, the same traditions and doctrines that the most conservative hold dear. They are not to be considered rebels, mere innovators—least of all, Protestants. They see the possibility, almost the inevitability, of the needed development in the very genius of their Church, that is, in its most honored traditions and doctrines.

Unity through "Return"?

Cardinal Ottaviani presided at the opening of a diocesan course in theology at Cortina d'Ampezzo in August, 1961. He is the head both of the Sacred Congregation of the Holy Office and of the Theological Commission for the Council. He was reported by "Osservatore Romano" (August 2, 1961) as having said that concessions could be made to those who might return to the Church. Once those truths were accepted from which no retreat is possible, returning sons would find their mother Church generous in liturgical, spiritual, and humane fields.

Such sentiments have become almost a stock in trade. They merit attention as an indication of a certain concern for wider Christian unity. As an inducement to return, much would depend on the extent, the timing, the form and manner, and the spirit of the proffered concessions. Pope John has declared that the house must first be put in order, renovated, purified, if it is to attract those who have not resided there for centuries.

An ardent advocate of Christian unity is Fr. Charles Boyer, S.J., of France, long associated with the Gregorian University in Rome. He was the prime mover in founding Roman Catholic "Unitas" soon after the close of World War II. During a brief period he sought and had the co-operation and counsel of a number of Protestants in Rome, including the present writer. Father Boyer seems more inclined to adhere to the idea of "return," even in the Octave of Unity prayers, than to the less determinative idea of "reconciliation" favored by the late Abbé Couturier (also of France) and incorporated in the prayers of the 1962 Octave.

Encouraging in tone and spirit is a recent word from Paul-Emile Cardinal Leger, Archbishop of Montreal, in a pastoral letter to his flock, reprinted in *The Catholic Mind* (April, 1962). In a paragraph on "Prayer for Unity," the Cardinal wrote: "All our human ambitions must be cast aside, and our prayer must blend with the intentions of the Lord, whose ultimate objective is the unity of all Christians in one Church, *in some mysterious way which we do not yet understand*" (italics added).

Where the Ecclesiastical Gap Seems Narrower

Relations with Eastern Orthodox and Anglican churches occupy a sort of middle ground, as compared with relations with most Protestant churches. Those who believe that this middle ground represents the territory most favorable for the next advance toward Christian unity can find considerable cause for encouragement. Pope John has frequently expressed interest and cordiality toward the Eastern Orthodox Church. Many Orthodox feel that he has not always drawn with care the line between the Oriental churches which adhere to the pope and those which have remained under Orthodox patriarchates. Many Catholics thought that the Pope was building a bridge for reconciliation with the Eastern Orthodox when he used the Greek rite in consecrating an archbishop of the Oriental rite within the Roman Catholic Church. Some Orthodox, on the contrary, feared that this was a bridge which portended invasion of their domain. (See further, Chapter 7.)

It was an important mission that took Archbishop Fisher, then head of the Anglican communion, to Rome to pay a courtesy call on Pope John late in 1960. Their agreement on the need for unity of spirit and for the spirit of unity was significant. But each sought to guard against drawing unwarranted conclusions from the episode.

There are Catholics who do not foresee the adequate development of Christian unity by piecemeal return of churches or individuals, and who therefore are concerned with the attitude of the Pope, the Council, and the whole Church toward the "separated brethren."

Actions Favoring Unity

Here one may derive more encouragement from the Pope's actions than from his words. In his words, he speaks primarily of the return of the separated brethren to a reinvigorated church. Pope John is perhaps somewhat handicapped here by the deaf ear which was turned to the appeal for unity made by Pope Leo XIII in 1897. Also, it may not be too easy to make a complete about-face from the encyclical "Mortalium Animos" of 1928, which discounted the ecumenical movement. Pope John has spoken rather generally about the ecumenical movement and certain meetings which have been held, making no specific mention of the World Council of Churches that has come to this writer's attention. But he has set up a Secretariat for Promoting Christian Unity which has operated with considerable freedom during the long period of Council preparation.

The Pope has also spoken of affirmative social goals, particularly of world peace. Christianity obviously requires much more unity than is now manifest in order to pursue those goals actively. The Pope recognizes this fact and has emphasized that the renewal of the Church and the return of the separated brethren to it must take place before those temporal goals can be achieved. The Pope has also emphasized doing the truth in a spirit of unity (Ephesians 4:15, 16). He has suggested that this would be an appropriate inscription over the door of the assembly. He has called for the reading of the Bible and for patience. He has spoken frequently of the need for the laity to be actively integrated into the Church's efforts, and has created a Commission for the Apostolate of the Laity, both religious and social.

Cardinal Agagianian

Gregory Peter XV Cardinal Agagianian is one of Catholicism's more noted champions of Christian unity. He is president of the Commission on Missions, one of the bodies charged with the preparation of the Council. He is the best-known Roman Catholic of an Oriental rite and prefect of the Sacred Congregation for the Propagation of the Faith. The Cardinal, who expressed some of his views to this writer, strongly supported Pope John's warning against expecting a "Council of union." The Council in Rome, he said, must be rather "the evangelizer of unity." For the Church of Christ to be a confederation in which each community confesses its Lord in its own way is not enough, he holds: nothing less is required than "the unity foreseen by the Gospel." But the times are changing, he noted; asperities are diminishing, and the atmosphere is propitious for a vast effort. But the Vatican Council is not a suitable forum for debate with the dissidents, he said, agreeing with Pope John that a Council of that sort could reach no conclusions, and quoting the Pope's statement, "Today perhaps more than ever the door to enter [the Church] is a narrow one."

"Osservatore Romano"

An indication of the strength of the traditionalists is to be found in the contrast between the Pope's appeal for "aggiornamento" and some recent items and articles in the semi-official Vatican organ "Osservatore Romano." A careful reader called to the author's attention three items —not as exceptions but as all too typical—that appeared in the single issue of January 25, 1962, exactly three years after Pope John's announcement of a Council that would, among other things, prepare the way for Christian unity:

1. The bishops receive their authority *through* the pope. (Roman Catholic theologians generally consider the bishops direct successors of the Apostles, the pope being the "guarantee," but not the "origin," of church unity. For example, Roman Catholics recognize Orthodox bishops as true bishops, though their authority is not received from the pope.)

2. A 1938 statement by Cardinal Della Costa was reproduced with praise, urging Roman Catholics to stay far away from non-Catholics, even in social life, since contacts with heretics are harmful to the Christian conscience.

3. Attributed to Saint Catherine of Siena (rightly?): "It is completely useless to look for Jesus in prayer or in the Bible; He is among us; it is the Pope."

In the next chapter we shall listen to the voices of Catholics who are trying to spell out the implications of the Pope's call for "aggiornamento."

5. *Bringing the Church up to Date*

It is said by well-informed Catholics that it is more difficult to determine the source of semi-official statements under Pope John than it was under his predecessor Pius XII. It has not been possible for the author, an "outsider," to discover who brought about the publication by "Osservatore Romano" of the famous "Firm (or 'Fixed') Points" in June, 1960. Only the Council's actions can reveal the relative strength of those who would hold the line and those who would heed the summons of the Supreme Pontiff.

Pope John's appeal for "aggiornamento," bringing his Church up to date, making it more effective in dealing with the twentieth-century world, has served as a stimulus or justification for many challenging suggestions by cardinals, bishops, theologians, and laymen. As the reader scans a few of these, he should bear in mind, remembering the seemingly contrary spirit reported in Chapter 4, that the author has no way (perhaps no one has) of estimating the effect on the Council of either the cautious or the challenging voices. The existence of the challenges is a significant fact which the Council will not ignore, both because they reflect facts that must be faced by all Christians and because many of the "challengers" are members of the Council. Even more significant than the challenges to the Council, is the uplifting of such voices within Roman Catholicism. As an American Catholic lay-man remarked in private conversation, there are currents flowing that no one can stem, not even the Council!

An archbishop, strategically related both to a congregation and to a commission, spoke to the author with evident satisfaction of the challenging leadership of Central European prelates. The same currents are evident in Holland and Belgium, and to a lesser extent are supported by some of the hierarchy in France, Great Britain, and the United States. This does not mean that Catholics in Italy, Spain, Portugal, and Latin America are isolated from twentieth-century pressures, but that so far their vocal leaders appear in general to rely on responses which seem to them to have been adequate in the Middle Ages. Perhaps two circumstances help to explain the phenomenon: those Catholics have long relied on a vast statistical preponderance and have traditionally been in control of the government, or at least supported by it. One Catholic symposium, *The Church and the Nations* (Sheed & Ward, 1959), a study of minority Catholicism in fourteen countries, suggests that the Church has more to fear from Constantine (that is, the embrace of the state) than from the persecution by Nero.

Some Belgian Voices

A group of French-speaking theologians centering at Louvain issued, late in 1960, a collection of studies entitled "Qu' attendons nous du Concile?" (What do we expect from the Council?) It is remarkable for its boldness in reporting an inquiry among Catholics, for its consideration of the separated brethren, and for its emphasis on current concerns. It has not gone unnoticed in Council preparations.

The foreword of the Louvain study declares that a new age confronts the Church. Among the ills of the world are mentioned inequality, the Communist menace, and a population growth that is outrunning the growth of missions and the number of religious vocations. A wide desire for the union of the Christian confessions was noted. All the faithful must express themselves, it was said, in order that the Council should be truly the voice of the whole Church.

One of the studies referred to a Council as "the continuation and the most adequate representation of the College of the Apostles." The Second Vatican Council must clarify doctrine and purify the Church and bring it up to date. These tasks do not call for a major demonstration, it was said, but for an act of humility. Current problems—with which non-Roman Councils deal through pronouncements—are usually treated by the pope in encyclicals, that is, letters to the bishops. For the sake of the true public image of the Church, according to the author of this study, it may be well to have the Council express itself on some of them. The Council, he said, must examine the whole concept of the Church: juridical, hierarchic, supernatural. It should also, following Pope John, emphasize the pastoral role, equalize resources, capitalize lay capacities, consider the role of priests in an industrial society—show to the world not so much a church triumphant as a church militant and suffering according to the example of Christ.

Considered Challenges from Germany

A young Swiss theologian teaching at Tübingen, Germany, Fr. Hans Küng, has written on *The Council, Reform and Reunion* (English edition, Sheed & Ward). The original German edition had a laudatory foreword by Cardinal Koenig of Vienna; the French edition, one by Cardinal Lienart. A writer in *Clergy Review* has called it a "must" for educated Catholics. An Anglican, commenting privately on Roman Catholic publications that share "the great hope of an ecclesiastical reformation in the same evangelical and ecumenical sense as indicated by Pope John," finds Father Küng's book "the best and most complete."

The Roman Catholic Church, according to Father Küng, is in its human aspect reformable. In that aspect, he finds that good classical qualities of imperial Rome have been exemplified in the Church. But along with them he finds in the "inheritance" a tendency to a policy of power, exaggerated legalism, formalism, authoritarianism. Among corrections that should be made by the Second Vatican Council, Professor Küng mentions:

Supplementing the definition of the pope's authority by clear definition of the rights and duties of bishops and councils.

Emphasizing the "pastoral" and "fatherly" role of the hierarchy, while diminishing the "bureaucratic" and "juridical."

Reminding Catholics that the Bible occupies the first and central place in the theology and teaching of the Church, and that the Liturgy centers on the Lord's Supper of the Gospel and the early tradition.

Putting the cult of Mary in a perspective that will guard against popular exaggerations.

According to Father Küng, the Church is to be renewed through suffering, through prayers, through the use of criticism, and through action. Separated brethren share both in the suffering due to the divisions among Christians and in prayer for unity. They should also share in criticism provided it is mutual and intended for each other's correction. Important steps, says Father Küng, have been undertaken during the past seventy years through honest dialogue. But there are important matters still to be cleared up. Catholics must understand that the Protestant Reformation arose out of genuine religious concern. The Holy Scriptures must be both further clarified by theologians and made the property of the people. Worship must be further domesticated and popularized if the ancient sense of a universal priesthood is to be recovered. Nations must be denationalized; the papacy must be further depoliticized. There must be a beginning of the reform of the Curia. There must be a growing understanding of toleration, and of the importance of the individual conscience.

Father Küng takes note of formidable obstacles in the way of the needed changes, but does not find them insuperable. God is ready; the human members of the Council must dare.

Following Pope John, Father Küng sees the necessity of successive small steps: neighborly acquaintance, followed by a closeness due to understanding, then perfect unity; but that, says Father Küng, would not be uniformity. The process must not take non-Catholics piecemeal—divide to conquer; for example, he says, "a re-

union with the Orthodox to the detriment of the Protestants would be pointless." The volume and earnestness
of expectation is such that the Council *must* not dis-
appoint it; yet the only firm basis for hope, says this
young theologian, is the work of the Holy Spirit.

Cardinal Frings of Cologne, speaking to the German
bishops in the summer of 1961, emphasized the need to
speak to the men of our time in their language and
praised the laity for their (indirect) participation in the
preparation of the Council.

Archbishop Jaeger of Paderborn welcomes the reformation of the canon law, as promised by Pope John,
feeling that the nature and structure of the Church itself
is what the Council most needs to clarify, putting the
roles of hierarchy and laity in their rightful places.

For the function and contribution of Augustin Cardinal Bea, also German, we refer the reader to Chapter 8.

A Daring Italian

Fr. Riccardo Lombardi, S.J., founder and leader of the
"Movement for a Better World," enjoyed the friendship
and strong support of Pope Pius XII. His book "Concilio—
per una riforma in carita" (Council—for a reformation in
charity) appeared only at the beginning of 1962, when
the Central Commission was already well along with its
evaluation and co-ordination of the work of the preparatory commissions. He followed Pope John most faith-
fully in his first two hundred pages. Most of his proposals
are considered to be no more radical than those of Father
Küng.

When, however, in the second half of the book, he
questioned whether an Italian is always the best choice

for pope, whether the Curia may not be an inadequate reflection of the world mission and membership of the Church, whether seniority promotion and life tenure guarantee the best leadership—whether, even, a lay "senate" might not provide a better representation of the Church—he was sharply taken to task in an unsigned article in "Osservatore Romano." This rebuke, in turn, was considered unfair and exaggerated by many Catholics. A mild call for prudence in making suggestions was uttered by Pope John after Father Lombardi had declared his unwavering obedience and his regret for the commotion caused by his book. He did not withdraw his suggestions.

Additional Notes

Catholic editors and publishers in the United States have provided much material on the Council and the ecumenical movement, original or in translation. Besides the Küng book, we note histories of general councils by Msgr. Philip Hughes, Father Murphy, Father Dvornik, Dr. E. I. Watkin, and Hubert Jedin; a handbook and commentary on the Second Vatican Council by the French academician Daniel-Rops; a booklet by Fr. Gustave Weigel, S.J., on issues affecting Catholic-Protestant understanding; and one by Fr. Gregory Baum, O.S.A., of Canada, on Christian unity in the teaching of the popes from Leo XIII to Pius XII.

Orientation through Commissions

A brief look at some of the preparatory commissions will help one in guessing what the Council will do, and in understanding what it actually does. The Commission for the Apostolate of the Laity, the Commission on Ceremonies (established after the June 5, 1960, announcement), and the Secretariat for Promoting Christian Unity do not have counterparts among the congregations that are part of the Curia. Nine commissions have each been headed by the cardinal who is chief of the corresponding congregation. There will be further consideration of the Secretariat in Chapter 8.

The Theological Commission

The Theological Commission may well prove to have been the most significant of the eleven. It is headed by Alfredo Cardinal Ottaviani, who likewise presides over the Congregation of the Holy Office. It is in this commission that any important theological proposal bearing on tolerance would have to originate. In the early fifties, the names of Cardinal Ottaviani and Cardinal Segura of Spain were often associated with statements and measures restricting the freedom of Protestants. Pius XII, in his famous address to Italian Catholic jurists in December, 1953, authorized a *political* deviation from their policy, under certain conditions, having first taken pains to round out the *doctrine* on which their policy was based.

One can hardly suppose that any doctrinal support has been found for regarding Protestant churches as sister churches. But Christian pluralism is a fact that can't be ignored in practice; Pope Pius XII took note of it in the 1953 statement. That statement is generally recognized— even, the author was assured, in the Sacred Congregation of the Holy Office—as papal teaching. Catholics deeply concerned for tolerance hope that the Council will be able, on theological grounds, to make a strong statement on freedom of conscience. This would undergird what might be done for religious liberty on grounds of policy, supported by other preparatory bodies.

In its theological statements, the Council will also influence the cause of unity, either by what it says or by its silence. It could move the Roman Catholic Church further along the road in developing the role of the Virgin Mary, tending to make her not only a mediatrix, but a coredemptress. Pius XII is said to have considered such developments premature. Many Catholics would regret such a step for two reasons. It would tend, they hold, at least in the popular mind and worship, to withdraw attention from the unique role of the Son. It would obviously widen the gap between Protestants and Catholics. By failing to go beyond the dogmas already defined with regard to the Virgin, or by some fresh statement of her role in revealing the richness of God's love for his creatures, the Council could leave the way open for further study and interconfessional conversations.

On the doctrine of infallibility, the Council might find a way to support the thesis that infallibility is guaranteed to the Church as a whole through the guidance of the Holy Spirit. Many Catholics would hold that this thesis is not contradicted by the definition of papal infallibility promulgated nearly a hundred years ago by the First Vatican Council. Such a thesis was stated by Fr. Francis Dvornik in *The Ecumenical Councils*, 1961, with the customary permission of church authorities. It might be stated by the Council in a way that the Eastern Orthodox Church would approve, and with which Protestants would find it difficult to take serious issue. Such a statement had been prepared for adoption by the First Vatican Council in 1870, the interruption of which prevented the completion of its agenda.

The Commission on Missions

Christian unity and religious liberty are each intimately related to the work of missions in non-Christian lands—by which one means those lands in which Christianity is not the principal religious orientation. Cardinal Agagianian, quoted in Chapter 4, is the head of both the commission and the congregation that deal with missions. Much of the conviction that the whole Christian cause is endangered by divisions and controversies has been brought to the home churches, Catholic and Protestant, by their foreign missionaries. Protestants have exported geographical and historical and national differences, at least in their labels. Northern and Southern Baptists, Methodists and Presbyterians, Lutherans, Anglicans, Congregationalists, Adventists, Church of God—what a kaleidoscope, not even an ordered spectrum, for the adherents of the millenary religions of the Orient, or the primitive worshipers of Africa!

But the Protestant-Catholic fissure is often even more confusing and hurtful to faith, because it goes deeper, and bridge-building or comity meets stouter ecclesiastical resistance. The Commission on Missions, naturally, is aware of all these factors and sensitive to them; that is certainly true of the Cardinal and the staff, who serve both Congregation and Commission. One gets the impression however that they have had their hands full, as a commission, with internal and administrative matters, and have been willing to leave to other preparatory bodies and to the Council itself the knotty problems of interconfessional relations on the missions fields and the development of tolerance, as far as Council action is concerned.

The Commission on Oriental Churches

Another commission that has been to some extent involved in interconfessional relations, especially with the Eastern Orthodox, is the one on the Oriental churches. It has been headed by Amleto Cardinal Cicognani, now also secretary of state since the death of Cardinal Tardini. The Oriental churches may be thought of as Eastern worshipers within the Roman Catholic Church. Many of them use the Greek rite in their worship; some of the clergy are married. They are known as Uniats, and include the converts to Roman Catholicism from the Orthodox, Armenian, Greek and other Eastern churches, as well as those of the Greek or Eastern rite who have long acknowledged the supremacy of the bishop of Rome. Each of these churches is headed by its own patriarch, as the Eastern Orthodox churches are, but they are all under the pope.

It is a good question whether the Uniats constitute a bridge or a barrier. In Southern Italy and Sicily, where they are rather numerous, they are not always thought of by their neighbors of the Latin Rite as true Catholics. On the other side, the Eastern Orthodox think of them as being estranged from the true Church, the Orthodox. It seems to have aroused suspicion and resentment among some Orthodox when Pope John, in the spring of 1961, used the Greek rite and language in consecrating Archbishop Coussa. Yet the Uniats are evidence of the

kinship in faith and worship between those who followed
Rome and those who followed Constantinople. Perhaps
they constitute a sort of Exhibit A for the invitation to
the separated brethren to "return." Just what role this
commission and congregation have played in preparing
the Council to deal with Orthodox relations is not easy to
discover. They, at any rate, make no suggestion that the
path to reunion is a simple, short, or easy one. One of the
staff of the Congregation related, from his own experience
on visits to Greece, how, in his opinion, the Orthodox
there are still burdened with the memory of eight hundred years ago. Then, during the Crusades, Western
Christians were found to be very troublesome guests—
somewhat on the order, one gathers, of the post-Civil
War carpetbaggers in America. These old wounds must
be healed, he felt, before meetings of pope and patriarch
or carefully drawn formulas could work to reunite the
two confessions.

Commission for the Apostolate of the Laity

In the June 3, 1961, issue of the national Jesuit weekly
America, Fr. Yves Congar, of France, remarked—along
with other important observations—that the layman as a
Catholic is priestly in completeness of dedication and can
more directly permeate the temporal life than the priest.
The upper clergy, he said, are even more fenced off from
places where men speak freely.

Many Catholics and other Christians will look with
hopeful concern for any Council encouragement for a responsible role for the laity. One of the consultants for the
Commission, pledged to secrecy as to its specific actions,
was nevertheless able to assure the author, both in April,

1961, and in January, 1962, of the consultant's encouragement by the spirit and proceedings in the Commission,
in line with Pope John's appeals for "aggiornamento."

A look at the Commission for the Apostolate of the
Laity is also appropriate in considering the possibility
that the Council will not be unduly dominated by a
largely Latin Curia. Fernando Cardinal Cento, the head
of this commission, is not responsible for the conduct of
a counterpart congregation; there is none dealing solely
with affairs of the laity. This commission can have a vast
indirect effect on church-state and Catholic-Protestant
relations. There was some reassurance, therefore, in a
statement that Cardinal Cento made to the author in the
spring of 1961. He was asked how his commission would
interpret the Pope's appeal for fitting the Church to work
in the modern world and prepare the way for the manifestation of Christian unity. He replied that he would
comment on a single point; that his own experience was
widely international, since he had served as papal nuncio
in several countries for a record total of thirty-three
years; that the members and consultants were drawn
from many nations; and that he could give assurance that
the orientation of the Commission would not be exclusively Latin. A note on Latin Catholicism will help to
make it clear why the Cardinal emphasized the widely
representative character of his commission.

Latin Catholicism

In most of the Latin language nations, the Roman
Catholic Church has been intimately allied with the
state, or the men of state, from the nation's origin. Only
in France and Italy did a political anticlericalism become

effective nationally for any considerable period. Even Mussolini became politically Catholic. In Italy are many devout Catholics who are politically anticlerical, but the Christian Democrats still hold uneasy sway; millions shudder at the thought of escaping the Fascist frying pan only to succumb to the Communist fire. In general, Latin Catholics, especially the Spanish and Italian clergy, have had little reason to develop a modern theory or practice of church-state relations, or to take religious pluralism or Protestants seriously. Nor have they had, until recently, much reason to pay attention to their own laymen. It is not surprising if, by and large, they seem more complacent, less responsive to contemporary needs and desires, than their counterparts in northern Europe, Great Britain and North America. Catholics are watching, therefore, to see whether the Latins—understood in this context—will dominate the Council as they have long dominated the Curia. Others may well look here, also, for one of the keys to the understanding of Council action. It was pointed out to the author by a consultant for one commission and by two members of the staff of another that the membership of the preparatory bodies was reassuring in this respect. In the Curia, as listed in the 1961 pontifical yearbook, there was found to be only *one* non-Italian name for two Italians; in the 1960 list of members and consultants of the bodies preparing for the Council, for each two Italian names there were *three* non-Italian.

The Central Commission

The Central Commission has considered the recommendations of commissions and secretariats, evaluated and co-ordinated them, and communicated the resulting agenda or "schema" to the bishops. The Council can modify the agenda. The First Vatican Council in effect ignored the preparatory materials, which, however, had been available in advance to only one-fifth of its members. They had not had the care, over a long period, of so widely representative a group of churchmen as is the case with the present agenda. Some two hundred bishops have been involved in the preparations. The Central Commission is composed of sixty-five cardinals and patriarchs from some thirty countries (about twenty-five resident in Rome), twenty-seven archbishops, six bishops, four superiors general of orders, plus twenty-nine counselors. The corresponding body for the First Vatican Council consisted of nine cardinals, members of the Curia, and eight consultant professors of ecclesiastical disciplines. (Statistics derived from "Civiltá Cattolica," 1961, pages 634-35.)

Bernard John Cardinal Alfrink of Utrecht has spoken of the responsible manner in which this pivotal commission conducted its work. Dissent had to be specifically justified—not merely "for reasons of my own." He and others have spoken of the fraternal atmosphere pervading the group. Its work has involved six or seven plenary meetings and vast travel mileage for the majority not resident in Rome. At the January, 1962, meeting, there were eight full sessions of three hours each, besides "homework" and committee meetings. Cardinal Alfrink has suggested that regular meetings of a similarly constituted body in the years after the Council might be useful. Other authoritative Catholics indicated to the author at least tentative support for the idea, and saw no canonical or traditional bar against it.

When the Council Assembles

In order to deal both thoroughly and expeditiously with a vast and complicated agenda, it is expected that the Council will divide itself into work groups, corresponding in general to the preparatory bodies. The nucleus of each group would consist of those who had participated in the corresponding commission or secretariat, whose knowledge of what had been discussed and rejected, and why, will obviously be most helpful to their colleagues—nine-tenths of the membership of the Council, who were not in the preparatory bodies. It has also been indicated to the author that the work groups will be able to benefit by the continued help of their members and consultants who have no voice in the Council itself.

6. "Separated Brethren" and the Council

Who are the "separated brethren"? How have they re-acted to the announcement and preparation of the Second Vatican Council? To be Christian brothers in the sense of the seven ecumenical councils of the fourth to the eighth centuries, it is clear that all must be evangelical, catholic, orthodox, and always ready to receive new light under the leading of the Holy Spirit. In Chapters 3, 4, and 5, we have looked especially at Roman Catholics. Chapter 7 is devoted principally to the Eastern Orthodox. In this chapter we shall call attention to other large international families of churches, to those who consider themselves evangelicals par excellence, and to the councils of churches whose development is so notable a feature of the Christian history of the past fifty or sixty years. This is not identical with the Protestant Church spectrum. The councils of churches increasingly include the Orthodox. Not all others who participate in the councils wish to be called Protestants. And there are many Protestants who have evinced no interest either in the Vatican Council or in the wider ecumenical movement.

The Anglicans

The separation of the Church of England from the Church of Rome was due, in considerable part, to personal and political aspects of the reign of Henry VIII.

Protestant emphases were powerfully asserted under Cromwell, but the separation can perhaps be said to have become final only with the accession of William III. Political features were also present in the Reformation on the Continent, but the changes associated with the names of Martin Luther and John Calvin were more doctrinal than the upheaval in England.

Many Anglicans, particularly of the Anglo-Catholic party or movement, prefer not to be called Protestants; they feel nearer to the Church of Rome than to those who bear the general label of Protestants, which most of the children of the Reformation accept. But the world-wide decennial assembly of Anglican bishops, the Lambeth Conference, includes those of the branch in the United States. There, the Triennial Convention voted, in 1961, to retain the title "Protestant Episcopal Church." Anglican ordinations are not regarded by Rome as satisfactory. Anglicans do not submit to the rule of the pope; they too are among the "separated brethren." Anglican national bodies are active members of the World Council of Churches. The Church of England is actively associated with the free, non-established Protestant churches in the British Council of Churches. In the United States, similarly, the Protestant Episcopal Church plays an important role in the National Council of Churches, and provided its first president.

The Church of England has long cultivated and maintained close spiritual ties with Eastern Orthodox churches. The Archbishop of Canterbury, Dr. Geoffrey Fisher, now retired, visited Ecumenical Patriarch Athenagoras in 1960. His successor at Canterbury, Dr. Michael

Ramsey, in 1961 called for renewed theological discussions with the Orthodox. (See Chapter 7.)

In the early 1920's Cardinal Mercier and Lord Halifax led a series of discussions at Malines that explored theological issues. In the minds of some of the participating Anglicans, they were a sort of pre-union exploration. They evidenced the possibility even then of free and serious dialogue. They also gave occasion for Cardinal Mercier to say that individual conversions did not constitute the only approach to reunion.

Other International Church Families

Baptists, Congregationalists, Disciples, and Methodists each maintain world-wide contact among the national or regional bodies of the given confession or family. The same is true of Presbyterians and Lutherans, whose world organizations have offices at the same address as the World Council of Churches. No direct approach by any of these six groups to the Vatican Council or to the Secretariat for Promoting Christian Unity has come to the author's attention. Dr. Pradervand, the secretary of the World Presbyterian Alliance has said (Religious News Service, January 23, 1962) that the WPA has no wish "to become involved in areas where the WCC can speak and act in the name of all Christians." He observed, however, that following the Second Vatican Council there might be a question for the WPA of conversations with the Roman Catholic Church.

Mergers

Within families of churches and across family or confessional lines, various mergers have been accomplished in recent years, are now in process, or are being proposed. In the United States, Lutherans, Methodists, and Presbyterians provide examples of reducing the number of denominations bearing the same family name. The United Church of Christ now includes churches of what were four denominations not long ago.

As crossing family lines, are to be noted the formation of the Church of South India and similar mergers in Canada and Japan. Under discussion is the possibility of the union—as a beginning—of Presbyterian, Methodist, Protestant Episcopal, and United Church of Christ denominations in the United States. Such drawing together of Protestants has no direct relation to the Vatican Council, but has a large influence on the climate in which it must work.

"Evangelicals"

Not all Protestant denominations affiliate with councils of churches, but their various relations to Christian unity and their attitudes to the Vatican Council are of great interest and importance. In some cases, the congregations being regarded as the important church units, the denomination as such has limited authority, though some of its boards may be very strong. Councils are feared by many Protestants as steps toward a superchurch. Some fear a movement toward Rome, or, more general and more basic, sacrifice of truth on behalf of unity—a unity that, on such terms, would be partial and illusory.

Among the effective promoters of church councils have been church leaders imbued with a passionate concern for social justice. The churches, they believe, would not be fully relevant to men's needs, especially in an industrial society, if their gospel were only individual and otherworldly. Nor would denominations or congregations, even with an otherwise adequate presentation of the Christian message, be effective in opposing the evils of society, they have held, unless they united their efforts. Council critics, when not insisting that the churches have no call to "meddle" in business and politics, often feel that evangelical truth is being neglected for the sake of social effectiveness.

The non-affiliated denominations have also an affirmative witness of great importance. Some of them insist on their evangelical character. To be Christian is, as we have noted, to be evangelical, just as it is to be catholic. Since either or both emphases are susceptible of being neglected or underemphasized, all Christians need to be reminded of them. The non-council denominations also assiduously guard the authority, the theology, and the ecclesiology which they find in the Bible.

Some of the Protestants outside the councils seem to be quite indifferent with regard to the Second Vatican Council. Some are hostile, apparently, to the Roman Catholic Church as a whole. Some are merely skeptical as to the Vatican Council's moving very far in the directions indicated by Pope John. Some Protestant theologians who are not active in councils of churches are contributing searching articles to the wider ecumenical dialogue.

Fairly representative of the attitude of non-Council Protestants in the United States is the following statement by Dr. Carl F. H. Henry. It was published in *Christianity Today* (April 10, 1961), of which Dr. Henry is the editor;

it was his reply in a survey conducted for Religious News Service by the present writer:

> The Protestant Reformers viewed the papacy as the height of human pretension. Against Roman Catholicism they championed the authority of supernatural knowledge (the inspired Scriptures) and the reality of supernatural salvation (justification by faith in Christ's mediation alone). In the twentieth century, Protestant ecumenism has made unity its prime interest, while Roman Catholicism emphasizes creeds and the authority of church tradition. Protestant liberalism meanwhile has blurred both scriptural authority and the doctrine of justification. Pope John XXIII's Second Vatican Council may be expected to express the desirability of Christian unity and the role of the creeds and church tradition, while avoiding the question that troubled the Protestant Reformers.

The Councils

It can scarcely be assumed that leaders of the major denominations participating in the National and World Councils of Churches are less evangelical than those outside these councils. Nor are they seeking union on Roman Catholic terms. In the author's survey for Religious News Service, what seems a cry from the heart was received from one well-known leader in the council movement; from this we quote an excerpt:

> In the most general terms I would hope that the Catholic Church would come out of its shell of isolation and rediscover the nature of its task in order to bear a relevant and effective witness to the gospel in this second half of the twentieth century. It needs to abandon its reliance on deductive reasoning from principles far removed from the living experience of this generation and learn to think and

act existentially. It needs to repent of its pride and folly in claiming special prerogatives on the grounds of a revealed mandate which the world at large does not take seriously, and to demonstrate the reality of that mandate by becoming anew the embodiment of the suffering, cross-bearing servant of God in the likeness of its Master. It needs to back away from the logically and historically untenable pretense of papal infallibility and to take a fresh grip on reality. It needs to sweep away the mythology of saint worship, Mariolatry, and other substitute faiths and to lay hold again on the infinite significance of the fundamental Christian affirmation: Jesus Christ is Lord.

I suppose no council is apt to do much of this, or perhaps any of it. But apart from such basic reformation what future is there for Roman Catholicism? And as long as Roman Catholicism is one of the major presentations of Christianity in the world, how can the pure gospel, uncluttered and unalloyed with all these irrelevancies, get a hearing?

Cautious Hope for Unity—not Union

Many Protestants who would agree substantially with the above nevertheless have indicated limited hopes that may not be entirely beyond the bounds of realism. In the survey mentioned earlier, nearly three-fourths of the Protestant replies revealed a cautious optimism. Some based it on hopes of action by the Council itself; some saw good results coming from the mere fact that Pope John wanted a Council and was preparing to hold one. Half the hopes expressed centered on encouragement by the Council for interconfessional conversation and for co-operation on practical problems.

Wide interest was expressed in the development of

improved relations between Rome and the Eastern Ortho-dox Church. Concern for religious liberty characterized a large proportion of the survey responses. Several men-tioned the Bible and increased study of it, possibly from an English language text acceptable to all Christians, as a factor in developing Christian unity. Even some of the barriers that seem insurmountable may be more in the way of church union than of Christian unity, for example, the cult of the Virgin Mary.

And Religious Liberty

In the Religious News Service survey, Protestant re-marks on religious liberty referred mainly to Protestant disabilities in Spain and Latin America. These vary from a kind of local ostracism to national legal discrimination and rest upon a close interweaving of religious, social, and legal factors (not always without a contributing irritation on the part of some Protestants). Hope was expressed that Protestants might come to be treated as well in those predominantly Roman Catholic countries as Catholics are in the United States; the Vatican Council could help. Catholics frequently say that such expres-sions as "Error has no rights," and "We'll accept treat-ment on the basis of your principles, but treat you ac-cording to our principles when we have the power," do not adequately represent their Church. Protestants would welcome a clear statement by the Council. This, said one, might well include "a reaffirmation of the doctrine of freedom of conscience in terms of the nature of God and his relation to his children" and their relation to each other. Tolerance, another recognized, is more secure if based on a real feeling of brotherhood.

That is, Christian unity, to be effective, must not only be accepted as a logical consequence of having one name and essentially one doctrine; it must be felt, and its practical consequences must not be denied or obstructed. "Separated *brethren*" must take the place of "*separated* brethren" in both the lay and the clerical emphasis. Some replies indicated that a noticeable shift in that direction is taking place.

For Individuals Only?

But others pointed out that the shift is still mainly at the individual level. It is very difficult, logically and psychologically, for the Catholic to speak of sister churches. There are evidences that it is easier to treat them so than to call them so. Perhaps, to use Dr. Norman Pittenger's phrase, we are nearing the point where Catholic thinking and action will include Protestant churches in the "corpus Christianum" (body of Christians), even though they can't yet bring themselves to include them in the "Corpus Christi" (Body of Christ), that is, the true Church.

Indirect Approaches

Thinking and feeling as they do, Catholics—including Pope John—frequently speak of the "return" of the separated brethren, to the no small discomfort of the latter. Some therefore look for viable but indirect paths to unity, to be trod perhaps with short and tentative steps. More frequent and friendly conversation, at all levels and on all subjects, is needed. The Council could both encourage and, to some extent, clarify and orient the process, which already has official sanction.

Several replies contemplate an improvement of relations between the Roman Catholic and Eastern Orthodox churches through the work of the Vatican Council, with benefits expected for the total ecumenical movement. The question was raised whether, on the contrary, closer relations there might not impede the growing understanding and co-operation between the Eastern Orthodox and Protestant churches. (See further, Chapter 7.)

A suggested road to increased unity is the selection of a few major and urgent world problems and concerted work toward their solution by all the churches. Peace, food for all, and racial justice suggest themselves. The same process is suggested at a community level, involving careful study of the given community and of the nature of a community.

The late Phillips Packer Elliott expressed hope for "recognition" by Roman Catholics "of the Reformation experience, amounting almost to awareness of its inevitability." A permanent study commission, he thought, might contribute to understanding of the past and so facilitate the Protestant-Roman Catholic dialogue. Deeper understanding is needed! A dozen years ago a Roman Catholic apostle of unity asked the author, privately and sincerely, why, since the scandals that provoked the Reformation had been eliminated by his Church, the Protestants did not return to it.

Councils of Churches

Side by side with church union developments, has been the growth of councils of churches, local, regional, national, and international. These have been a response to the practical need for co-operation and, to some degree, a corrective reaction to the kaleidoscopic panorama of denominations—in general, a submission to "the coercions of history," as at least a strong indication of the leading of the Holy Spirit. While some see in the conciliar movement, as it might develop, an adequate manifestation of Christian unity, others fear that its good might become an obstacle to the best, a way station mistaken for the destination.

The World Council of Churches was formally constituted in 1948. It can be thought of as the confluence of two movements and two series of world conferences of Protestant churchmen, known respectively as "Life and Work" and "Faith and Order." Its identifiable ancestry goes back at least to the 1910 Edinburgh conference on Christian missions. The joining of the International Missionary Council and the WCC in 1961 further identified the missionary and conciliar movements.

The National Council of the Churches of Christ in the U.S.A. has, from its foundation, had as one of its four major sections the Division of Christian Life and Work, which was to a large degree the heir of the forty years' experience of the Federal Council of Churches. Only recently did the NCCC provide officially for a department of Faith and Order. This should facilitate more effective participation in the wider ecumenical movement.

Both the World Council and the United States NCCC now include different branches of the Eastern Orthodox Church. The Russian, Romanian, Bulgarian, and Polish Orthodox Churches applied for membership in the World Council of Churches in 1961, and were accepted at the meeting in New Delhi.

The WCC and the Second Vatican Council

The attitude of the World Council to the Second Vatican Council, and its response to the new opportunity connected with it, is indicated by the action of its Central Committee, meeting at St. Andrews in Scotland in September, 1960—very soon after the announcement by Pope John of the creation of a new secretariat to confer with non-Roman Catholics on questions in the field of unity. (See Chapter 8.) The following statement by the Central Committee is taken from the *Ecumenical Review* of October, 1960 (pp. 45-46).

From the point of view of the WCC, this development is important for various reasons. First of all, it shows how much has happened since the Vatican made its first official statement on the ecumenical movement in the encyclical "Mortalium Animos" of 1928, which contained a wholly negative interpretation of the movement. There is little doubt that in the meantime the Vatican has come to see that the ecumenical movement is not inspired by a vague humanitarianism, but by basic Christian convictions. Secondly, the Vatican has now decided to become active in the ecumenical conversation. Thus—to use a phrase of Father Congar—for the first time in history the Roman Catholic Church, on the occasion of the Ecumenical Council, enters into a structure of dialogue.

The full meaning of these developments will only become clear in the coming years. But we can say this much at the present time:

a) The fact that a dialogue with the Roman Catholic Church becomes possible is to be welcomed.

b) It is to be hoped, however, that this new development will not mean that the informal discussions which have been going on between Roman Catholic theologians and those of other churches will henceforth be entirely superseded by more official discussions, for at the present stage it is precisely the informal discussions which can best contribute to the removal of misunderstanding.

c) No church should fear that the WCC will in any way seek to act or speak for its member churches in matters concerning church union. The WCC is, according to its constitution, not authorized to act for the churches in such matters. In these matters each church takes its own decision in full freedom. This is for us an obvious point. But it must be made because the question is sometimes raised whether the WCC will enter into formal or informal conversations with the Roman Catholic Church about church union. The answer is that this is quite out of the question because of the character of our movement.

d) The WCC may, however, use such opportunities as may present themselves to make known to the new Secretariat certain basic convictions which have been expressed by the Assembly or Central Committee (e.g., issues of religious liberty, of Christian social action, etc.).

e) It should be remembered that the creation of the Secretariat does not mean that any of the fundamental differences which exist between the Roman Catholic Church and the churches in the WCC have been solved. The change is a change in procedure and in climate. The opportunity for dialogue is to be grasped, but it means that the real problems will come to the fore. Our task in that dialogue will be to represent the insights which God has given us together in the fifty years since our movement was started.

Clarification by the General Secretary

Further light on the role of the World Council in the total Christian ecumenical movement is afforded by the following comments of its General Secretary, Dr. W. A.

Visser 't Hooft, in his report at St. Andrews to the Central Committee (*loc. cit.*, p. 56), under "Relationships with the Roman Catholic Church":

> If I analyze the present situation correctly, the road which the WCC will have to find in this respect is the road between two abysses. The one danger which we will have to avoid is that we should consider ourselves or become generally considered as an opposite number of or a counterweight to the Roman Catholic Church. . . . We must remind ourselves and others that the WCC is a body *sui generis* which refuses to become the adversary of any church or group of churches, and stands for unity in Christ of all who recognize him as God and Saviour.
>
> On the other hand, there is the danger that in order to facilitate contacts with the Roman Catholic Church we should give up convictions and principles which belong to the very essence of our movement. In saying this I think particularly of the advice that a certain number of Roman Catholic ecumenists are giving us. This advice amounts to saying that the one and only valid activity of the WCC is theological study and conversation about the issues of reunion of the Church. Everything else is considered by them as a dangerous deviation from the true task of the Council. Now we have made it abundantly clear that full unity is and must be the goal of the WCC, but we believe, at the same time, that there are urgent common tasks to be performed even now, and that the performing of these tasks will help us to advance toward unity. We come from Edinburgh and Stockholm as well as from Lausanne, and we are not ashamed of any of our ancestors [that is, movements identified with Missions and Life and Work, as well as Faith and Order].
>
> There are other things in our living tradition which we are not prepared to give up for any price—our convictions

about religious liberty, our concern for an ecumenical relationship between the churches in which there is a real listening to each other.

To avoid both dangers will take much wisdom and patience. But the purity of our cause is at that price.

The WCC, in its New Delhi assembly late in 1961, continued the orientation of St. Andrews. World Council leaders, not expecting giant steps toward Christian unity by the Second Vatican Council, are prayerfully hoping for a net contribution. This would consist of small steps tending to clarify differences and remove misunderstandings, and would be a clear indication that continuing interconfessional conversations have the support of the Roman Catholic Church as a whole. Aware of the existence and vigor of the seemingly less ecumenical and less developmental currents noted in Chapter 4, they are not inclined to be too optimistic with regard to the Council itself, as distinguished from results already visible from the calling of the Council, the processes of preparation, and the creation of the Secretariat for Promoting Christian Unity.

7. The Eastern Orthodox Churches and the Council

When one considers certain words of some who speak as Roman Catholics and some who speak as Eastern Orthodox, one feels that these ancient confessions are at the very threshold of reunion. Then one turns to equally sincere and representative words from others in both camps and feels sure that only the millenium will see the closing of the breach. One is speaking now, not of church members, but of churches. One senses much more of impending drama—with positive or negative denouement almost equally conceivable—than in the case of Catholics and Protestants or Protestants and Orthodox. What are some of the elements in a situation so unpredictable? How can one be in doubt whether to expect a rapid closing of a schism that is usually dated from 1054, or another mutual frustration such as occurred after the Councils of Lyons and Florence? (See below.)

Several of the modern popes, notably Leo XIII, have shown concern for reunion with the Orthodox. Pope John has on many occasions uttered cordial and hopeful words concerning them and his desire for healing the schism. Ecumenical Patriarch Athenagoras, from his palace in Istanbul, has voiced corresponding sentiments, and has spoken most highly of Pope John personally. But a frequent Catholic visitor in Orthodox territory has reported privately that much more is needed, to bring reunion, than a new formula or an embrace of the prelates.

How Did the Separation Come About?

Writing in 1954 of the causes of the schism, Archimandrite (now Bishop) Emilianos Timiadis refers to a "pentarchy" in the first centuries after Emperor Constantine had freed the Christians and established a patriarchate at Constantinople—namely the sees of Rome, Constantinople, Alexandria, Antioch, and Jerusalem. Pope Gregory I, he says, "recognized the equality among all the (five) patriarchs," claiming precedence but not jurisdiction; the five formed "an administrative federation, of which the Emperor constituted the point of cohesion."

One may speak with propriety of unity of faith and worship among the Christians of the five patriarchates as long as they recognized and submitted to the same general or ecumenical councils. But after Emperor Constantine removed the imperial capital from Rome to Constantinople, a patriarchate was created there. The emperor often thereafter played an important role in church politics, and the sees of Rome and Constantinople became involved in imperial politics. It was difficult at any time thereafter to speak of a fully united Church, although Christians throughout the Mediterranean basin formed a community, a fellowship whose members felt at one with each other.

Beneath the rivalries that began to appear were cultural differences. The East was Hellenized, speculative, concerned with worship; the West, Latinized, juridically oriented, activist. By the end of the ninth century, for example, the West had added a phrase to the creed saying that the Holy Spirit proceeds from the Father *and* the Son ("Filioque" in the Latin).

The Orthodox, with the spirit of tolerance that they call *oiconomia,* seem less exercised by the difference of meaning between the two formulas than by what they consider an arbitrary modification by the West of the work of fully ecumenical councils.

Except for Rome, the patriarchates, old and new, have tended to be national in scope and feeling, each closely identified with its people and, until recent decades, with the government. But when the Orthodox are accused of caesaropapism, subjection of Church to state, they remind us that early councils were convened by the emperor, and that the bishop of Rome allied himself with the emperor more than once to defeat a rival patriarch. (The same religion for ruler and people was the rule in Western lands until quite recent times.)

The Unity is Fractured

In the ninth century a very scholarly layman, Photius, was made patriarch of Constantinpole. Between him and the pope there was a prolonged struggle, with mutual excommunications, bargains, and renewed breaks. It was Photius who challenged the supremacy of Rome in both creedal and administrative matters. Until recently he was probably the principal sinner in Rome's eyes. Recent studies, for example, by Father Dvornik (of Czechoslovakia and the United States) have removed much of the traditional stigma; Pope John is reliably reported to be glad that Rome no longer has to put all the blame for the schism on Constantinople.

In 1054, Patriarch Michael Cerularius rejected and publicly burned a Roman bull that attempted to excommunicate him. The Roman legates had lost their authority while in Constantinople by the death of the pope before they composed the bull. But succeeding popes, who might still have healed the breach, sustained the legates.

An additional bar to any early reconciliation was furnished by the crusaders. Western nobles and prelates, traversing Orthodox lands on their way to recover the Holy Sepulcher from the Moslems, often were guilty of pillage and even conquests. Coming at the beginning of the thirteenth century as allies of the Eastern emperor, they ended by occupying and sacking Constantinople in 1204. Fr. Dvornik comments: "The atrocities perpetrated by the Latins in the conquered city and the desecration of Greek sanctuaries further widened the gap between Latins and Greeks." Constantinople was reconquered by the Eastern empire in 1261. But the indignities and injuries inflicted by the crusaders, and the papal pressures that ensued, are remembered by some Greeks, we are reliably informed, as though they had occurred only yesterday.

Medieval Attempts at Reconciliation

At the Council of Lyons, in 1273, Pope Gregory X secured an agreement with five ecclesiastical representatives of Michael VIII, the Byzantine emperor. Gregory was ready to support Michael against a threatened invasion and reconquest of Constantinople by Charles of Anjou, the ruler of Southern Italy and Sicily. The primacy of the pope and the procession of the Holy Spirit from the Father and the Son ("Filioque") were accepted by these legates. But the historical structure of the Orthodox Church provides that there must be consent of the broad body of Christians. The Greeks in Byzantium were far from reconciled theologically or politically. Moreover, Pope Gregory's successor, Martin V, supported Charles of Anjou, declared Michael schismatic, and decreed his deposition—a decree not honored in the East. Thus the Lyons "agreement" never took effect.

Again, at the Council of Florence, in 1439, an agreement seemed to have been reached that would have ended the schism. The formula was arrived at under political pressure on the Orthodox; the Turks were at the gates of Constantinople. But clergy and laity among the Orthodox were not prepared to compromise theologically or to forget ancient grievances, even though their representatives had helped formulate the agreement. Some said, "better the sultan's turban than the Pope's tiara!" So the formula was of no more effect than the one worked out at Lyons had been.

Continuing Barriers to Reunion

Profoundly important cultural and political differences between Rome and Constantinople, and very diverse patterns of church-state relations were enough, it would seem, to have brought about the schism. Those differences, as well as differences in theological emphasis, have persisted well into this century. Coupled with them is the dispute as to who was schismatic from the true Church.

But there is such external pressure on all Christian bodies, and such correspondence between Roman Catholic and Eastern Orthodox faith and worship, that the possibility of closer relations would almost certainly accompany the overcoming of major differences as to authority and unity.

Rome settled with apparent finality—for itself—the question whether *pope or council* has ultimate authority, when, in 1870, it defined papal infallibility. (The very calling of the Second Vatican Council seems to imply the possibility of a certain pragmatic flexibility in the exercise, if not the definition, of the pope's over-all authority.) The Orthodox would seem to have no insuperable difficulty, emotional or doctrinal, in accepting the pope as the "first among equals" (but not infallible) as a matter of traditional protocol, a matter of honor, not authority, among the patriarchs of autocephalous churches. But necessary doctrinal agreement is to be found, for them, in the acts of the seven Councils of the fourth to eighth centuries (325-787), which the Orthodox recognize as fully ecumenical—and any such that may meet in the future, provided, of course, that they do not theologically contradict the accepted seven.

Holding the differing convictions regarding authority and church structure that they do, it is not surprising that Catholics and Orthodox have correspondingly differing notions of Christian unity. For Roman Catholics, unity is only partial and relative apart from complete and organic union under the leadership of the pope. While each autocephalous church has its own patriarch, the Orthodox find the necessary unity in all having the same doctrine (accepted by truly ecumenical councils), and the same sacraments and Liturgy. Narrowing the difference between Eastern Orthodox and Roman Catholic views as to authority would almost certainly contribute to narrowing the difference as to unity, and vice versa. By calling a council, Pope John may have opened the door to a somewhat less inflexible Roman Catholic view of authority. By changing the titular concern of the new secretariat from "union" to "unity," he has implied that there is a reasonable distinction between the two—at least an interim one.

A Pan-Orthodox Meeting

The Ecumenical Patriarch and his predecessors have been active champions of all-inclusive Christian unity for several decades. But the patriarchates themselves exist among peoples very diverse in culture and politics. Invited by the Ecumenical Patriarch, representatives of thirteen of them came together on the Isle of Rhodes in the autumn of 1961—the first Pan-Orthodox meeting in many years. There were World Council observers and Roman Catholic journalists present. The following observations are based mainly on the unpublished account of an Orthodox participant.

The Rhodes meeting is reported to have been characterized by unity of spirit, attributable only to the Holy Spirit, and most triumphant in the most difficult moments. Both ancient and modern patriarchates were represented. The Russian Patriarchate, for example, dates only from 1448 (the Russian Orthodox Church, from 988).

Six topics were discussed in a preliminary way and put on the agenda for the Pro-Synod, which may not meet until after the Vatican Council. (The prestige of the Ecumenical Patriarch was maintained by, among other acts, leaving to him the call and the determination of the date of the Pro-Synod.) The topics and questions, briefly indicated, were:

1. Faith and dogma. Orthodoxy is pivotal for Christian unity. Do the Orthodox churches need to elaborate a formal confession of faith?

2. Administration and ecclesiastical order, including the role of the laity.

3. Relations among the autocephalous churches, including the affiliation and administration of the Orthodox churches of the modern diaspora. More generally, the problem is for the great patriarchates to preserve their unity and co-operate effectively.

4. Orthodoxy and social problems.

a) Is Orthodoxy limited to charismatic permeation of society, of the world? Or is it to study and formulate positions on specific social questions?

b) Given radically different political situations (for example, in Greece and in Soviet Russia), is ethical examination of the points at issue necessitated?

5. Relations with other ancient churches of the East. Churches of Malabar, Syria, and Armenia, and the Coptic churches of Ethiopia and Egypt were represented alongside the dozen autocephalous Orthodox churches. Interim exchange of delegations, discussion, and study will prepare for the Pro-Synod to discuss reunion with them.

6. Relations with the churches in the Christian world of the West. The Slavic-language patriarchates were preparing to join the Greek-language ones in membership in the World Council of Churches. (The Orthodox Churches of Russia, Rumania, Poland, and

Bulgaria were in fact accepted by the WCC two months later at New Delhi.) The whole attitude of Rhodes toward the WCC was affirmative.

To avoid or correct certain misinterpretations of the Rhodes meeting, we are informed that the Orthodox have "relations" with Rome and other Christian churches; they are "participants" in the World Council of Churches. Also, there was unanimity in according the chair of honor to the ecumenical patriarchate, and in including in the agenda certain politico-social topics proposed by the delegates of the Russian Orthodox Church: peace, disarmament, nuclear tests, race, colonialism.

It may be added that a competent Catholic visitor present throughout the Rhodes meeting reports that he found no occasion of offense in its general attitude toward Rome.

Confirming the almost traditional friendship between Anglicans and Eastern Orthodox, the Rhodes meeting favored the resumption of theological discussions between them. This had been suggested in a message to the conference by Dr. Arthur Michael Ramsey, Archbishop of Canterbury. Several such discussions between Anglicans and one or another national Orthodox church took place between 1930 and 1939, and were resumed in 1956. The 1961 Orthodox meeting in Rhodes recommended comprehensive resumption of them.

Some Orthodox Attitudes toward the Vatican Council

In an address on the Eastern Orthodox witness to unity at the New Delhi meeting of the World Council of Churches, Professor Nikos Nissiotis made clear the context in which an authentic Orthodox attitude toward the Second Vatican Council is formed and is to be understood (*The Ecumenical Review,* January, 1962). "In Orthodox thinking, Church union is an absolute reality pre-established by God . . . to be identified with the union of the Father and the Son (John 17:22-23)"—not an attribute of the Church, but its very life, he said; one moves from this union toward unity, not creating it, but recapturing it. Unity is found not in "subtle pseudo-theological formulas—but in the life of historic churches springing from the same source as the life received at Pentecost." The witness of Orthodoxy, pivot-church for the ecumenical movement, is one of patience, according to this distinguished lay theologian. "To use such slogans as 'come back to us' or 'let us go back to the first eight centuries' as though we were inviting others to deny their own traditions is unorthodox." Neither "the Roman schism nor the Reformation which resulted from it," he said, is to be classified as "outside the Church."

"We must hope and pray," the Professor continued, "that the Second Vatican Council will re-evaluate the diocesan system by a reinterpretation of the primacy of the Holy See in the full Catholic and Orthodox sense of *ex consensu Ecclesiae et non ex sese* (by the consent of the Church and not of itself)." "First among equals" was the status acquired by the bishop of Rome as "a response to the desires of the local churches for an initiative in convening pan-Christian councils and for a link between the churches such as the patriarchate of Constantinople provides for the Eastern Church today." "There are no schismatics, but the historic churches in their divisions represent a schismatic situation in the One Undivided Church." The unity we seek is "not that of a centralized authoritarian discipline, nor is it based only on the preaching of the gospel, but it is a charismatic and eucharistic unity, expressed through and for communion with the grace of God the Holy Trinity."

Orthodox spokesmen hold firmly to the principle that the Church is identified by the bishops as successors, collectively, of the Apostles. Since the Orthodox bishops are in the authentic apostolic succession, they are in no sense inferior to the Western bishops, and they hold that they could not attend an *ecumenical* council as mere observers; if it is ecumenical, they are an integral and necessary part of it. The Ecumenical Patriarch is willing to exchange visits with the Pope, but not to make a one-way visit that might be construed as paying homage. The Orthodox churches evidently see the road toward the necessary full consummation of Christian unity as being at present via the World Council of Churches, of which nineteen of them are members.

Writing in *The Ecumenical Review* of October, 1959, Professor Hamilcar S. Alivisatos said that before an eighth ecumenical council representing all Christians could be held, a long period of such work as that of the World Council of Churches would be required. That period would presumably resemble "the centuries before the Great Schism," when "a kind of co-existence was tolerated on both sides." To return to that state would mean a "kind of provisional solution, subject to God's further guidance."

The Orthodox are willing, even eager, to talk with Roman Catholics. But as late as June, 1961, they observed with something approaching bewilderment that the Secretariat for Promoting Christian Unity, which had been created for relations with all the "separated brethren," was taking no steps for conversations with the Orthodox, except as they were included in conversations arranged in co-operation with the World Council. Instead, they were left to infer that they might find liaison through an official in the Congregation for the Oriental Churches who was a Uniat. (See Chapter 5.)

In July, 1961, the Ecumenical Patriarch received visitors representing Pope John sent by the Oriental Congregation (which, according to reliable information, had been induced to act by Cardinal Bea, the head of the Secretariat). This relieved the frigidity of the atmosphere, but did not result in an invitation to send official Roman Catholic observers to the Rhodes meeting in the early autumn. Roman Catholic visitors, or reporters, however, were present at Rhodes.

With all the Orthodox Churches meeting together for the first time in many years, and with four more patriarchates joining the World Council of Churches, one may well believe that phenomenal progress toward the expression of Christian unity is being made by the Orthodox. Also, one may well wait and study developments at, and after, all the three great ecumenical gatherings before becoming unduly impatient: the World Council meeting at New Delhi, November-December, 1961; the Second Vatican Council, 1962-63; and the Pan-Orthodox Pro-Synod, date still uncertain.

One speaks of a Pro-Synod, or pre-Synod rather than Synod, because the Orthodox are consistent in their idea of an ecumenical Christian assembly. They hold that

Rome cannot hold an *ecumenical* council without the Orthodox. They will not consider their own assembly truly ecumenical without Roman Catholics.

Meanwhile, there are some less intransigent voices among the Orthodox with regard to relations with Catholicism. The Jesuit Journal in Rome, "Civiltá Cattolica," in its August 19, 1961, issue, reported the views of eight well-known Orthodox theologians and prelates, Russian, Greek, and Syrian-Antiochian. The reviewer, Fr. Paul Leskovec, S.J., points out that the views noted were privately expressed. He sees a ferment in Orthodoxy, and a divergence in their opinions as to the nature of the Church, which he ascribes to their being, in effect, sheep without a shepherd, but he is encouraged by Orthodox reactions to Pope John's calling of a Council.

Catholic Voices

Representatives of Orthodox autocephalous churches met in Moscow in 1948 to celebrate the 500th anniversary of the autocephalicity of the Russian Orthodox Church. They listed many scores of Roman Catholic publications that "spread among the Latins unprejudiced information, full of brotherly love, about Eastern Christianity even though it is separated from Rome." Many of these publications, they said, had been aided in the twenties and thirties by Pope Pius XI.

Pope John XXIII served for years as papal nuncio in countries where Orthodoxy is the major Christian confession. He has mentioned his desire for unity and union with the Orthodox much more often than he has referred to Protestants in a similar connection. He has presented himself to the Eastern Church as "your brother."

Cardinal Amleto Cicognani, soon after becoming the Pope's secretary of state, reviewed the historical conditions that led to separation. Since these have now changed, he said, "there is no reason why such an unfortunate state of separation should prevail."

Fr. Christopher Dumont, Dominican, editor of a French-language bulletin, *Toward Christian Unity*, commented shortly before the Rhodes gathering on the visit to the Patriarch in July, 1961. The Roman authorities, he said, had not taken public notice of the "profuse marks of attention and sympathy" emanating from the Ecumenical Patriarch during the preceding and present pontificates. This silence, he wrote, could not fail to astonish the Patriarch. The July visit, in Father Dumont's opinion, had "dissipated this slight cloud in a way that could not fail to touch profoundly the delicate heart" of the Ecumenical Patriarch Athenagoras I. Father Dumont then hoped that the visit would result in the presence of Roman Catholic observers at Rhodes. In any case, he said, conversations of a most fruitful nature would now be possible, even if private and on the fringe of official meetings. He remarked on the vastly increased significance of a pan-Orthodox meeting that included representatives from the Iron Curtain countries. (Father Dumont had earlier commented favorably on the application of the Russian Orthodox Church to enter the World Council of Churches.)

Another writer in the same bulletin, *Toward Christian Unity*, Father Le Guillou, also a Dominican, in the summer of 1960, reviewed several factors in the new surge of the Orthodox toward manifesting their own unity, and concluded that it would be a favorable factor in promoting unity talks between them and Roman Catholics.

Père Louis Bouyer, writing in the spring of 1961, found the barriers between Catholicism and Orthodoxy more apparent than real. He quoted Cardinal Siri to the effect that the collegiality of the bishops has been and still remains regardless of councils, the traditional way of the Catholic Church. To show that this need not be interpreted as something said to woo the Orthodox in view of the coming Council, Father Bouyer quoted from an unnamed "one of the most eminent authorities of the Holy Office, two years before Pope John's accession," who said that union between Orthodoxy and Catholicism "already exists under a curtain of misunderstandings and reciprocal ignorance." It will be manifested when "on both sides one ceases to present different but inseparable perspectives as contradictory. . . ." (Compare with the foregoing statements by Profs. Nissiotis and Alivisatos.)

What Might the Vatican Council Do?

How can the Vatican Council deal with questions raised by the Orthodox in a way that will begin to restore fraternal relations and at the same time not impede the wider ecumenical movement?

It can provide for continuing contact and conversation to remove misunderstandings and clearly define differences. For example, while Rome feels generous in receiving millions of "Uniats" with their ancient language, liturgy, and customs practically intact, this is regarded by the Orthodox as an invasion—unwarranted, unfriendly, and unseemly. Contacts with the Orthodox might be put in the hands of the Secretariat for Promoting Christian Unity. If effective co-ordination of all such contacts is provided, piecemeal reconciliation will be less likely to take precedence over the total ecumenical concern, and the left hand will be less likely to frustrate the right.

If the Council makes the collegiality of the bishops more than a convenient phrase to be summoned once a century (it almost certainly will), it will reaffirm a link with Orthodoxy not offensive to most other Christians who wish to pursue unity. And if, at the same time, it finds a way to affirm or imply that infallibility rests in the whole Church, guided by the Holy Spirit, it will begin to undo some of the harm and remove some of the misunderstanding traceable to the interrupted First Vatican Council, which also met at St. Peter's, nearly a hundred years ago.

8. Union and Unity:
A Council Perspective

The most notable single step on behalf of Christian unity that Pope John has taken since his announcement of the Second Vatican Council has been, in the author's judgment, the creation of The Secretariat for Promoting Christian Unity (official English title). What it has already done will vitally affect Council action. What the Council recommends to Pope John with regard to the continuance and support of the Secretariat could be an important index to the orientation of the Council. A look at the Secretariat will help to obtain a proper perspective on the Council.

The Secretariat for Promoting Christian Unity

Pope John XXIII said of the Secretariat on June 5, 1959, when he announced it, along with the preparatory commissions for the Council:

> As a token of our affection and good will towards those who bear the name of Christians but are separated from this Apostolic See, to enable them to follow the work of the Council and to find more easily the path by which they may arrive at that unity for which Jesus Christ prayed so earnestly from his heavenly Father, we are establishing a special "advisory board," or secretariat, presided over by a cardinal whom we shall choose, and organized in the same manner as the commissions.

Augustine Cardinal Bea, of Germany, the only cardinal who is a Jesuit, was named the next day to head the body. Before the end of June, Msgr. J. G. M. Willebrands of Holland was appointed as secretary. Voting and consulting members and staff were named later. Among them are: Fr. James F. Cunningham, a Paulist, a voting member; Msgr. John M. Oesterreicher; Fathers Gustave Weigel, S.J., George Tavard, A.A., and Edward Hanahoe, S.A., consulting members—all from the United States; and Fr. Gregory Baum, O.S.A., of Canada. Another American Paulist is Fr. Thomas F. Stransky of Milwaukee, one of the assistant secretaries; the other assistant secretary is Msgr. Jean-Francois Arrighi, of Corsica.

The Secretariat states that it has a double purpose. Its immediate purpose is to give accurate information to non-Catholic Christians concerning the work of the Council; also, to hear and weigh their suggestions and pass them on, if need be, to the appropriate commission or draft them for consideration by the Council itself. That is to help the Council in promoting Christian unity. But its larger and more general end is to aid non-Catholic Christians in their pursuit of the unity for which Christ prayed, according to the situation in various lands.

The Secretariat has held several plenary meetings. In addition, members and staff have been constantly busy, privately and publicly, preparing and promoting the Council's work for unity. It co-operated with leaders of the World Council in setting up a consultation of several days near Geneva in May, 1961, on religious liberty. Orthodox, Protestant, and Catholic theologians—some twenty in all—explored each other's minds, exchanged views, and discovered how much they had in common and where and why they differed. Such a meeting was in accord with the statement issued by the Central Committee of the World Council of Churches at St. Andrews in September, 1960, reported in Chapter 6.

Archbishop Fisher has said that his visit to the Pope would have been impossible if the Pope had not created the Secretariat. It was the Secretariat, also, that *chose and authorized* the Roman Catholic observers sent to the meeting of the World Council of Churches in New Delhi. The president of the Secretariat, Augustin Cardinal Bea, eighty years old and vigorous in mind and spirit, is an internationally known biblical scholar, with wide personal contacts with non-Catholics. Since his appointment, he has traveled extensively in America and western Europe, speaking often, and warmly welcomed by Protestants and Orthodox as well as Catholics.

In an unhurried conversation with the author in the spring of 1961, Cardinal Bea emphasized his interest in religious liberty. The Cardinal referred to a conversation he had recently had with a South American prelate, as evidence of the lack of ecumenical orientation of both Protestant and Catholic church members and lower clergy in some areas, where church leaders wish to promote tolerance. There is the additional difficulty, the Cardinal noted, of distinguishing properly in practice between legitimate, obligatory Christian witness and an unbecoming proselytism.

More recently, speaking in Paris, Cardinal Bea has referred to the importance which Christian reunion will have on the agenda of the Second Vatican Council, which may pave the way to an eventual assembly of Christian bodies under Roman Catholic Church auspices to discuss unity. Ruling out compromise on dogma, he found room for much clearing up of misunderstandings that have arisen because of the historical circumstances in which declarations of dogma were made. More profound biblical and historical study is needed, he said, for example, of the mystical Body of Christ. He cited Pastor Marc Boegner's conviction that those things which unite Protestants and Catholics are greater than the differences (RNS, January 29, 1962).

In February, 1962, Monsignor Willebrands, the executive leader of the Secretariat, visited the Orthodox Ecumenical Patriarch Athenagoras I in Constantinople, and the newly elected Greek Archbishop Chrysostom in Athens. Orthodox sources indicated that the question of observers at the Vatican Council was discussed, but that action on a still hypothetical invitation would be taken only after discussion by the holy synods involved.

Other Secretariats

On the initiative of the Roman Catholic Archbishop John Carmel Heenan of Liverpool, a national secretariat for promoting Christian unity has been set up. It has been widely publicized, and favorable Protestant reactions are reported. Similar secretariats were reported, as early as January, 1962, in France, Holland, northwest Italy (home of many Waldensians), and Madagascar. Recently, a commission for ecumenical concerns was established by Archbishop Lawrence J. Shehan of Baltimore, the primatial see of the United States. A notable feature of this commission is the inclusion of two laymen. Cardinal Cushing indicated that he would create a similar body, and Archbishop Jaeger of Paderborn did so—

the Johann-Adam-Moeller Institute. These bodies, not officially connected with the central secretariat in Rome, are both an evidence of ecumenical concern on the part of many Catholic leaders and an instrument for promoting dialogue between separated Christians.

Union and Unity

The Imperative. The Christian ideal is recorded in the prayer of Christ himself in his last evening with his disciples before his trial and crucifixion.

> I do not pray for these only, but also for those who are to believe in me through their word, that they may all be one; even as thou, Father, art in me, and I in thee, that they also may be in us, so that the world may believe that thou hast sent me (John 17:21-22).

But the ideal, for centuries past, has failed of realization. Catholics, Orthodox, or Protestants may affirm that the ideal is embodied in their church, and strive earnestly and honestly to make it true, but the manifestation is less than convincing to other Christians, still less to a skeptical world. But for many decades now there have been widespread stirrings in all the Christian confessions and increasingly vocal demands and formal actions calling for a more determined and united approach to the goal. Multitudes of Christians—not all—are increasingly impatient of their outward divisions.

United effort by Christians in opposing temporal evils was never more needed, surely, than now; abundant evidence has been cited in preceding chapters. Ignorance, hunger, the menace of a nuclear holocaust: they have their spiritual dimensions too! In view of the need, both temporal and spiritual, Pope John might well have used the language of an earlier age when he called a Council to prepare the way for a more effective Christian unity: "God wills it!"

Pope Pius XII is reported by Daniel-Rops to have drawn up a "schema" of two hundred pages on the unity of Christians. Pope John is known to have had a major concern for unity, especially with the Eastern Orthodox, for at least the past fifteen years.

What Kind of Unity?

What kind and degree of unity is needed most urgently? What can the Council be expected to do about it? Unity will not be adequately achieved or perfectly expressed, most Christians would probably say, until all are united under one confession of faith, one name, one church government. Union would be the result, eventually, of the efforts of the World Council of Churches. Its chief executive, Dr. Visser 't Hooft, said in 1961 that the churches ought to regard their present form and status as provisional. The prevailing official voices in the Church of Rome call for union through the "return" of all Christians to their mother Church. The Orthodox offer effective union, they say, with separate patriarchates, not essentially different from each other. What are the advantages, the perils, if any, and the difficulties in the way of formal and complete union?

One big Church with a central administrative authority would have tremendous power, prestige, and mobility for action. It would have great spiritual appeal for those who abhor disorder, find theological disputes distasteful, and seek a kind of coziness not to be found in the present divided state of Christians. If it were really permeated with the Christian virtues and graces, and thus had inward unity as well as outward union, it would be truly "the Body of Christ." Its value as a demonstration and its attractiveness as an invitation would be vastly increased.

Except as its leaders and members should become saints, however, one big Church would be exposed to the danger of the corruption that is invited by power, and the complacency that comes with security. That these are not imaginary perils could be illustrated by many examples, local and national, where a church has had, or thought it had, a monopoly. The examples are not confined to any one of the confessions. They are not confined to formally established, state-supported churches. A local church may "run" a community, dominate a school board or a town hall.

Those who think and work and pray for the progress of the wider ecumenical movement must realize that union without unity would be unreal, superficial, illusory. They also agree, from all the major confessions, that none of them is in fact yet ready for union. But some direct steps toward that far-off event have been taken, and others are under serious consideration. Such are the reunions and mergers of churches to which reference was made in Chapter 6. In each case, one may assume, there is a sufficient fact and feeling of unity to induce and maintain the union. All the churches learn from the experience of these few.

Why So Slow?

Why has union not gone forward more rapidly? Within Protestant ranks, local churches and whole denominations keep their servants so busy with budget, planned programs, intra-Protestant competition, and a host of other things, that too little time and energy are left for thinking of the Christian cause as a whole. Many feel sincerely that the larger concern is, and must remain, beyond human wisdom and power. Some are not displeased to remain divided. The inertia of habit and the halo of tradition impede both thought and action. In many cases, mutual trust between persons and denominations has not been developed to a point where it would be useful to plan for union. And there are the very real conviction that one's church is organized the right way and the fear that something precious and unique would be lost from the faith by any merger.

Language and ethnic barriers have also been important obstacles to Protestant reunion, both internationally and within the United States, where generations have been required to bring together members of the same family of churches who come from different lands. But the development of councils of churches and the lasting effects of the movements on which they have been built are now more rapidly removing or overcoming historical and cultural obstacles. More attention can therefore be given to deeper differences in doctrine, order, and worship. The councils have thus become one channel of unity and one symbol of advance toward whatever union is divinely intended.

The Eastern Orthodox patriarchates have not until recently again been uniting their efforts in a way to satisfy themselves, chiefly because of cultural and political differences among the nations with which they are identified. Willing to leave to the state far more of what

Catholics and many Protestants conceive to be religious concerns, the Orthodox have felt less need to unite their efforts for social purposes. It is still early to estimate the effect of Orthodox emigrations to western lands, the new contacts among the Orthodox patriarchates, and increasing Orthodox membership and participation with Protestants and Anglicans in national and world councils of churches; all these seem to be assets, or to afford opportunities, in the struggle for Christian unity. More than forty years ago the ecumenical patriarch of that day sounded a call for Christians to unite.

And Roman Catholics? Their official statements offer only to welcome the separated brethren when they "return to the Father's house." But they are putting great stress on the need for Christian unity. They have recently emphasized anew that individuals may be Christian though outside the Roman Catholic Church. The denial of this doctrine by Fr. Leonard Feeney of Boston a few years ago was the occasion for his excommunication. The doctrine is sometimes supported on the ground of the non-Catholic's "invincible ignorance," a phrase that does not sound too fraternal to Protestant ears, but discloses a limited recognition of the unity of all believers. Pope Pius XII dwelt on the concept of the mystical Body in an encyclical entitled, from its opening Latin words, "Mystici Corporis," nearly twenty years ago. Statements recently current are to the effect that valid Christian baptism certainly relates one somehow to the Church, but in a fashion not yet adequately explored and surely not clearly defined. Cardinal Bea has recently suggested that this might be a proper subject for consideration by the Council.

The Roman Catholic climate is definitely "fairer and warmer" both in the widespread and deeply felt desire for more visible and more effective Christian unity and in the readiness to talk, officially and unofficially, with non-Catholics. It seems to be true that both the ecumenical spirit and the practical steps promise more ameliorations than can yet be forecast from the statements of officials.

Seeing that the Roman Catholic Church is taking such pains, and going so far, to promote Christian unity, it is natural to ask why it does not take one or both of two further steps. Why not speak of other churches as sister churches, and treat them as such? Definition would be difficult, but one finds unofficial references to "separated churches." Why not adopt the Orthodox practice of equal patriarchates, unity without formal, administrative union? This would be difficult, not to say impossible, to reconcile with the juridical supremacy of the bishop of Rome.

In times of war or other great stress the clergy of different confessions have been drawn very close in spirit and in co-operation. Something of the experience remains. Many Catholic laymen who understand the traditional and theological difficulty are nevertheless ready and eager to treat other truly Christian churches as part of their family of faith, and already think of them so. Mutual recognition of this kind would not immediately or automatically lead to the perfect unity that Pope John spoke of as the third stage. But it might make possible a sort of round table meeting, or series of such meetings, of the sort that have constituted the path for 197 churches into the World Council.

Perspective

As a reporter, the author at this point must sound a warning to the reader. From the ecumenically favorable indications reported here, one might be tempted to expect more from the Council than it is likely to do. Those who have been willing to talk with the author—Roman Catholic, Eastern Orthodox, Anglican, or Protestant— have in the main been those who at least want the Council to respond to the challenges laid down by Pope John. But even an accurate and complete study of all that has been said, officially and unofficially, concerning the Council would not enable one to forecast with any high percentage of certainty what the Council will do in those areas of greatest concern to Christians not officially participating in its deliberations.

Whatever the ecumenical currents may portend for the Second Vatican Council, they are flowing in the Roman Catholic Church, and around it. The call and preparation of the Council and the creation and work of the Secretariat for Promoting Christian Unity have opened the channels wider for Christian understanding and fellowship.

An ecumenical fellowship is growing around the world. It is a challenge to the churches, all churches, to reflect whether it is not indeed the stirring of the Holy Spirit.

Epilogue

"Ancient prejudices and bitternesses on both sides are dying down," Paul Emile Cardinal Leger of Montreal declared in a sermon recently, "and a genuine will to unity is becoming more apparent on both sides." Dr. Claud Nelson's perceptive reading of the meaning of the coming Second Vatican Council and the Association Press' gracious invitation to add a coda as a Catholic priest involved in the ecumenical enterprise is an illustration of the Cardinal's observation. Contacts are multiplying, friendships are forming, mutual trust is growing. In the United States—such at least is my impression—we are still largely in the pre-theological phase of the ecumenical discourse. "Dialogue has replaced diatribe" is Archbishop John C. Heenan's description of where we are. It is much to say after the separation of centuries and the bitterness of clashing loyalties. For a continuing conversation supposes mutual recognition of unprejudiced minds, sincerity, and intelligence; more, it denotes an acceptance of God's will for men as the supreme norm and their ultimate goal. To be indifferent to the unity with the Father and among his followers that was the first purpose and the final gift of Jesus Christ, his Son and our Saviour, is universally seen as treason to God's will.

Hence the Catholic interest in the World Council of Churches at whose Third Assembly at New Delhi last fall I was an official observer of the Holy See. Hence the

widespread interest among non-Catholic Christians in
the coming Second Vatican Council whose preparations
and perspectives and purposes Dr. Nelson describes so
sympathetically. This is normal and proper, for Pope
John XXIII has promised that the Council "will be profit-
able for those separated from this Apostolic See." To that
end, long before the convening of the Council and the
process of collating the 9,000 suggestions for its agenda,
the Holy Father created the Secretariat for Promoting
Christian Unity, a special organ paralleling the preparatory commissions. Its purpose, His Holiness declared, is
"to demonstrate our love and good will toward those
who equally bear the name of Christians . . . so that they
may also follow the work of the Council and more easily
find the way leading to unity." A typical reaction was
that of His Grace, Arthur Ramsey, Archbishop of Canterbury: "The present Pope seems to me to have a great
Christian good will and much love. And where love is,
the results are incalculable."

It is important that misunderstandings as to the function of the Second Vatican Council be avoided, an effort
that has preoccupied Dr. Nelson in his diligent research.
There is a very grave chance that the Council will leave
large disappointments if its scope is not recognized and
if the complications of its undertaking—the first corporate
meeting of all the Catholic bishops of the world in nearly
a hundred years—are ignored. As knowledgeable a man
as Giovanni Cardinal Montini, former Vatican pro-Secre-
tary of State, felt obliged to warn his people that the
Second Vatican Council "will not be a magic and immediate remedy for all the problems facing the Church."
In a pastoral letter the Archbishop of Milan noted that

the Church "intends to come into contact with the world by means of the forthcoming Council." His Eminence continued: "we are all interested, therefore, in its success, but we must guard against two illusions which could become disappointments for the future." The two illusions are the belief that the Council will be radical or revolutionary in its decrees and that it will fabricate the automatic solution of all the difficulties confronting the Church today.

The Second Vatican Council is not, as some imagined, a Council of Unity such as were the abortive efforts of the Council of Lyons in 1274 and of Florence in 1439, unhappy experiences which Cardinal Bea told an audience in Paris in February, 1962, counsel prudence in such matters. "Both resulted in the re-establishing of unity with the representatives of the separated churches of the East," His Eminence observed, "but this unity remained without result, the clergy and the faithful not having been spiritually prepared for it."

The work of the Second Vatican Council is directed primarily to Catholics. In his Lenten pastoral, Cardinal Cushing explained the reason: "For the evils of schism which have brought separation among those who call themselves Christians, we find the matching evils of pride and selfishness among those who have remained loyal to the jurisdiction of the true Church. We must put our own house in order if we would make possible the return of those whom we regard as wanderers. We must present to the world the image of the Church as Christ founded it if we would ask recognition from those who have sought Christ elsewhere because they have been unable to find him in the lives of Catholics." The sad

fact of a divided Christendom is present to the mind of
the Archbishop of Boston as he envisages the solemn
convocation of the bishops in St. Peter's Basilica on October 11: "As we celebrate the Eucharistic Liturgy which
will solemnly open the Council, these will present an
ample spectacle before the world of the serene unity
which the Church treasures and reveals. But this unity
even then will not be extensively perfect, not until all
Christian bodies unite in perfect harmony of faith and
join in that awesome Mystery of Faith which is both the
symbol of perfect unity and its divine cause—the Holy
Eucharist."

We are urged by St. Paul, we are directed by the
Holy Spirit: "By professing the truth in love, let us grow
in union with Christ who is the Head." Truth and charity are, then, irretrievably linked in the ecumenical task.
The secretary general of the World Lutheran Federation
sees this clearly: "The realization of the unity of the
Church has a possibility of success only if it is placed
flatly on the foundation of truth. Every other fashion of
aspiring to union which neglects the truth would also
achieve a fictional unity." The Catholic Church's charge
to guard the deposit of faith entrusted to her care makes
any compromise with truth, any reversal of declared
points of revelation out of the question. The Lutheran
Bishop of Hanover, Hanns Lilje, agrees that it would be
"unthinkable for a Council to put in doubt the dogmatic
bases of the Catholic Church."

But cultural encrustations can be exposed and different modalities of expression, the fruit of different philo-
sophical systems, explored. Theological language, shaped
by historical circumstances and so offering only a certain

aspect of a doctrine, can be re-examined so that the full profundity of the truth may emerge. "Humani Generis," the encyclical on the proper methods of theological inquiry, declared that "the two sources of divine revelation [Scripture and Tradition] contain such grand and such numerous treasures of truth that they could never be really exhausted."

Thus, the new emphasis on the historical and scientific, and even sociological, in theology and Scripture study opens new prospects for an impartial, objective, and methodically exact reading of the sacred Scriptures to learn which is the unity revealed by Christ as his will for the Church. In this sense, the Council may well address itself to a closer study of what is the Church and the relations of non-Catholics to it. Cardinal Bea has observed: "The question of the nature of the Church has been before us since the Council of Trent. But neither at that Council nor at the First Vatican Council has this fundamental question been able to be treated in a complete and profound manner. It pertains to the next Council to face this task made easier in our day, thanks to important studies of competent theologians and especially to the penetrating exposition of the Church as the Mystical Body of Christ in the encyclical of Pius XII. Qualified Protestant leaders concede that in that encyclical the nature of the Church appears in a form they have never before suspected."

There is a growing realization that the relation of baptism to membership in the Church needs further exploring. Cardinal Bea has noted that all who have been validly baptized in Christ, even outside the Catholic Church, have been, by the fact of their baptism, incorporated in

Christ and made children of God. His Eminence quoted with approval the words of Philip Maury, then general secretary of the World Student Christian Federation and now director of the Department of Information of the World Council of Churches, to the Pax Romana Congress, an international Catholic student organization, in Fribourg, Switzerland, last August: "Despite our ecclesiastical, theological, and human differences, we are brothers because we depend uniquely on the grace of our common Saviour, Jesus Christ."

Given the ancient, ample, and seemingly intractable difficulties separating Christians of good will, the realistic judgment of Professor Kristen E. Skydsgaard, a Lutheran expert on Catholicism, is well weighed: "The conclusive thing may not perhaps take place until the second, third, or fourth council which will follow this one." We should be encouraged, however, by the reminder of Monsignor Cassien, Rector of the Orthodox Theological Institute of Saint-Serge at Paris: "It is God who guides history. But the effort which he demands of us—an effort of study and of charity—this effort is, even in our separation, an expression of unity." Our efforts will doubtfully have results in our lifetime, but they will not for that reason be in vain: "I have planted, Apollo has watered; but it is God who has given the increase. . . . For we are co-operators with God" in a task he thought worth the life and death of his Son:

> *Redemisti crucem passus*
> *Tantus labor non sit cassus.*

Edward Duff, S.J.
Editor of SOCIAL ORDER